A READING GUIDE TO THE NEW TESTAMENT

—

DAVID H. MULHOLLAND

Deseret Book Company
Salt Lake City, Utah

To my wife, Lois,
to our children, David, John, Brian, Sarah, Roger, and Matthew,
for allowing me the time necessary to write,
and to others who have given me the benefit of their knowledge of
the New Testament

©1990 David H. Mulholland

ISBN 0-87579-386-X

Printed in the United States of America   72082-4667
10 9 8 7 6 5 4 3 2

Contents

Preface

This reading guide will help you study the New Testament so that you will better understand the life and teachings of the Savior during his mortal ministry. You will also come to understand some of the challenges the early Saints faced in maintaining a unity of the faith.

"A *testament* is a solemn covenant. The gospel is the Lord's testament (covenant) of salvation. When the gospel was revealed in the meridian of time, it replaced the old Mosaic covenant—an old testament which had been in force for some 1500 years—and so the new revelation was called the *new testament*." (Bruce R. McConkie, *Mormon Doctrine* [Salt Lake City: Bookcraft, 1966], p. 534.)

Speaking in particular of the Gospels, the first four books of the New Testament we have today, Elder McConkie said:

"They contain hidden and unknown treasures. We haven't caught the vision and come to realize what we can get out of the gospels. Would it surprise you if I suggested that there is more knowledge in the four gospels, more revealed truth relative to the nature and kind of being that God our Father is, than in all the rest of holy writ combined? All we need to do is learn how to get that knowledge out. We need guidance. We need the Spirit of the Lord to direct us as we study.

"It is not reading alone; it is reading, pondering, and praying so that the Spirit of the Almighty gets involved in the study and gives understanding." (*Ensign,* Apr. 1975, pp. 70–71.)

How to Use This Reading Guide

As you begin your study of the New Testament, first read the headnote to the chapter you are studying and then read the chapter itself. Refer to the footnotes as you read. Both the headnotes and the footnotes will help you understand better what you read in the chapter. They will also help you answer the questions in this guide.

Next, write in the guide the answer to each question and the number of the verse or verses where each answer is found. You will find most of the answers in the chapter you are reading in the New Testament, but you may need to look for a few answers in other places in the scriptures.

The designation "See" after a question refers you to the passage where you will find the answer. That designation is used only when the full answer is not in the chapter you are currently reading. For example, "See John 4:1a" after a question means that you will find all or part of the answer in footnote a to verse 1 of John 4.

The designation "See also" refers you to related information that is not necessarily part of the answer. For example, you may be referred to the Bible Dictionary, which is in the appendix to the Latter-day Saint edition of the King James Version of the Bible.

Compare the verse or verses you wrote down with the verses listed in the Answers section at the back of this book. The Answers section should be used as a guide; you may find some answers in other verses not listed there.

In addition to the scriptures and this guide, the New Testament student manual prepared by the Church Education System for the institutes of religion will help you better understand the history and doctrine you are reading: *The Life and Teachings of Jesus and His Apostles* (Salt Lake City: The Church of Jesus Christ of Latter-day Saints, 1979).

Questions about the Bible

Title Page

_____ a. What is the complete title of the Bible?

_____ b. What is the origin of the King James Version?

To the Most High and Mighty Prince James . . . : The Epistle Dedicatory

_____ a. By what titles did the translators of the Bible address King James?

_____ b. Why did the translators pay King James this tribute?

The Names and Order of All the Books of the Old and New Testament

_____ a. How many books are there in the New Testament in the Latter-day Saint edition of the King James Version of the Bible?

_____ b. List the five study aids in the Appendix.

Explanation Concerning Abbreviations

_____ a. Where are the listed abbreviations used?

_____ b. What does the abbreviation GR indicate?

_____ c. What does HEB indicate?

_____ d. What does IE indicate?

_____ e. What does JST indicate? In what two places are the excerpts to be found?

_____ f. Where can you find the abbreviations for books of scripture contained in the Bible?

_____ g. Where can you find the abbreviations for books of scripture contained in the Book of Mormon, the Doctrine and Covenants, and the Pearl of Great Price?

Introduction to the Bible

See Bible Dictionary, page 622, s.v. "Bible."

_____ a. What is the Bible?

_____ b. What is meant by the word *bible*?

_____ c. Who originally wrote the various books in the Bible?

_____ d. What are the two great divisions of the Christian Bible?

_____ e. In what languages was the New Testament originally written?

_____ f. What does the word *testament* mean in Hebrew?

_____ g. What is the Old Covenant?

_____ h. What is the New Covenant?

_____ i. How many books are in the Latter-day Saint edition of the King James Version of the Bible?

_____ j. What three kinds of evidence determine the text of the New Testament?

_____ k. What is the position of The Church of Jesus Christ of Latter-day Saints regarding the Bible?

_____ l. What did Joseph Smith teach about the Bible?

_____ m. What has the Lord given us to sustain, support, and verify the Bible?

See Bible Dictionary, page 624, s.v. "Bible, English."

_____ a. To whom does the "honor of making the first translation of the Bible into English from the languages in which it was originally written" belong?

_____ b. What happened to him in 1536? Why?

_____ c. How many years were required to translate the "Authorized Version"?

See Bible Dictionary, page 717, s.v. "Joseph Smith Translation (JST)."

_____ a. What is the Joseph Smith Translation?

_____ b. When was most of Joseph Smith's translation of the Bible completed?

_____ c. What might Joseph Smith have done "had he lived to publish the entire work"?

_____ d. What did the Prophet receive as a direct consequence of making his translation?

_____ e. What does the Joseph Smith Translation to some extent assist in doing?

_____ f. Why is the Joseph Smith Translation important to students of the scriptures?

See Bible Dictionary, page 630, s.v. "Canon."

_____ a. What did *canon* originally mean in Greek?

_____ b. What is *canon* used to mean now?

_____ c. What do we learn from modern revelation about the preservation of the books of the Bible?

_____ d. How did the Gospels come into being?

_____ e. What was the primary purpose of the epistles?

_____ f. List three rules that were used to determine the validity of certain writings as scripture.

_____ g. When and how will additions be made to the current collection of scripture?

Questions about the New Testament

Introduction to the Gospels

See Bible Dictionary, page 682, s.v. "Gospels."

_____ a. What does the word *gospel* mean?

_____ b. What is the good news proclaimed in the Gospels?

_____ c. List the names of the Gospels in the New Testament.

_____ d. Who was Matthew's record directed to? Why?

_____ e. Who does Mark direct his testimony to?

_____ f. What does Luke give his readers?

_____ g. Who was John writing to?

_____ h. What was the primary purpose of John's testimony?

_____ i. Why is it important to study all of the Gospels?

_____ j. What is the Harmony of the Gospels?

_____ k. On Map 14 in the Maps section of the Appendix to the Bible, find Bethlehem, Nazareth, and Jerusalem. (See C6, C3, C6.)

See Bible Dictionary, page 763, s.v. "Roman Empire."

_____ a. Which empire was the greatest power in the world at the time of Christ? (See Map 13.)

_____ b. What language was spoken in most of the empire?

_____ c. What were the three largest cities in the empire?

_____ d. How did the Romans treat national religions?

_____ e. What could the Jews do when an unauthorized person was found "inside the middle wall of partition" in the temple?

_____ f. What did the Romans do for the church Christ established during the first thirty-six years after the Ascension?

_____ g. What caused persecution of the Christians to begin in A.D. 64?

The Gospel According to St Matthew

Introduction

See Bible Dictionary, page 729, s.v. "Matthew."

_____ a. What does the name _Matthew_ mean?

_____ b. What was Matthew known as before his conversion?

_____ c. What kind of work did Matthew do before his conversion?

_____ d. With his knowledge of the Old Testament prophecies, what was Matthew able to see and understand?

_____ e. Who was his gospel written for?

_____ f. What was the chief object of his writing?

_____ g. What else does he emphasize?

Matthew 1

_____ a. How did Joseph Smith entitle the book of Matthew? (See footnote to the title, p. 1187.)

_____ b. Who was the husband of Mary?

_____ c. What do the Greek title "Christ" and the Hebrew title "Messiah" mean? (See Matthew 1:16e; see also Bible Dictionary, p. 633, s.v. "Christ.")

_____ d. How many generations were there from Abraham to David? From David "until the carrying away into Babylon"? (Matthew 1:17.) From "the carrying away into Babylon unto Christ"? (V. 17.)

_____ e. What did Joseph decide to do after he learned that Mary was expecting? (See v. 19b.)

_____ f. Why did Joseph choose not to divorce Mary? (See also Bible Dictionary, p. 608, s.v. "Angels.")

_____ g. How was the prophecy in Isaiah 7:14 fulfilled?

Matthew 2

_____ a. Who could the wise men from the east have been? (See Bible Dictionary, p. 789, s.v. "Wise Men of the East"; p. 727, s.v. "Magi.")

_____ b. Why did they come to Jerusalem?

_____ c. Where did King Herod send them? (See also Bible Dictionary, p. 621, s.v. "Bethlehem"; p. 700, s.v. "Herod.")

_____ d. What did the wise men do when "they saw the young child"? (Matthew 2:11.)

_____ e. Why did Joseph take Mary and Jesus to Egypt?

_____ f. What edict did Herod give about the children in Bethlehem and the surrounding area?

_____ g. Why did Joseph and Mary return with Jesus to the land of Israel?

_____ h. What information did Joseph Smith provide about Jesus' early years? (See v. 23c.)

Matthew 3

_____ a. Who came "preaching in the wilderness of Judaea"? (Matthew 3:1; see also Bible Dictionary, p. 714, s.v. "John the Baptist"; p. 725, s.v. "Locusts.")

_____ b. What was his message?

_____ c. What does the Greek word for *repent* mean? (See Matthew 3:2a; see also Bible Dictionary, p. 760, s.v. "Repentance.")

_____ d. What did the people who believed John's message do?

_____ e. What did John say to the Pharisees and Sadducees? (See Matthew 3:7d.)

_____ f. Who is Abraham, spoken of in verse 9, and what did God covenant with him? (See Bible Dictionary, p. 601, s.v. "Abraham"; p. 602, s.v. "Abraham, Covenant of.")

_____ g. What did John promise that the Savior would do? (See also Matthew 3:11a.)

_____ h. Why was Jesus baptized? (See also 2 Nephi 31:5–9.)

_____ i. Who bore record at Jesus' baptism that Jesus is the son of God?

Matthew 4

_____ a. Why was "Jesus led up of the Spirit into the wilderness"? (Matthew 4:1; see v. 1b.)

_____ b. What had Jesus done during his fast? (See v. 2c.)

_____ c. List the three temptations Satan spoke of to Jesus.

_____ d. Who did Jesus send to John when he was in prison? (See v. 11a.)

_____ e. What did Jesus begin to do after his fast?

_____ f. What did Jesus say to Peter and Andrew? (See also v. 19a.)

_____ g. What did Peter and Andrew do?

_____ h. What did Jesus do in all Galilee? (See also v. 23f.)

Matthew 5; 6; 7

VERSE NUMBER

_____ a. To whom was the Sermon on the Mount given? (See Bible Dictionary, p. 771, s.v. "Sermon on the Mount.")

_____ b. What two other sources help us understand the Sermon on the Mount? (See Bible Dictionary, p. 771, s.v. "Sermon on the Mount.")

_____ c. List the three main themes of the Sermon on the Mount as recorded in the book of Matthew. (See Bible Dictionary, p. 772, s.v. "Sermon on the Mount.")

Matthew 5

VERSE NUMBER

_____ a. What does the word _beatitude_ mean? (See Matthew 5:3a.)

_____ b. Who will be blessed?

_____ c. To what did Jesus compare the members of the Church?

_____ d. What did Jesus instruct us to do? Why?

_____ e. Who will be saved in the kingdom of heaven? (See v. 19b.)

_____ f. Who is "in danger of the judgment"? (V. 22; see also v. 22b.)

_____ g. What should be our attitude toward those who offend us? Why?

Matthew 6

VERSE NUMBER

_____ a. Why should we give to the poor in secret?

_____ b. What does the word _hypocrite_ mean? (See Matthew 6:2a.)

_____ c. List three principles of prayer taught in verses 5 through 8. (See also Bible Dictionary, p. 752, s.v. "Prayer.")

_____ d. List three things we are to ask of our Father in Heaven in our prayers.

_____ e. When will our Father forgive our trespasses?

_____ f. How should we fast? (See also Bible Dictionary, p. 671, s.v. "Fasts.")

_____ g. Why are we to lay up treasures in heaven?

_____ h. What is required for our bodies to be full of light? (See also Matthew 6:22b.)

_____ i. Why can we not serve both God and mammon?

_____ j. What is the promise for seeking first the kingdom of God? (See also v. 33a.)

Matthew 7

_____ a. What kind of judgments are we to make? (See Matthew 7:1a.)

_____ b. What are we to do before seeking to correct our brother? (See also v. 3a, b, c.)

_____ c. Why are we to be sensitive about the spiritual things we share with others? (See v. 6a.)

_____ d. What are the requirements for receiving blessings from God? (See v. 7a.)

_____ e. Where is Golden Rule found?

_____ f. Why are we to enter "in at the strait gate"? (V.13.)

_____ g. How will we know the true prophets from the false ones?

_____ h. Who will enter into the kingdom of heaven? (See also v. 21e.)

_____ i. Where does a wise man build? a foolish man?

_____ j. Why were the people astonished at the Savior's doctrine? (See also v. 29a.)

Matthew 8

_____ a. What did Jesus do for the leper?

_____ b. Who did Jesus say had great faith? Why? (See also Bible Dictionary, p. 632, s.v. "Centurion.")

_____ c. What did Jesus do for Peter's mother-in-law?

_____ d. What did Jesus do for those who were "possessed with devils" and those who were sick? (Matthew 8:16.)

_____ e. What did Jesus do during the storm to save the ship and those who were on it?

_____ f. How did the devils address Jesus when he came to them?

Matthew 9

_____ a. What does it mean to be "sick of the palsy"? (Matthew 9:2; see v. 2a.)

_____ b. What statement of comfort did Jesus make to the man who was "sick of the palsy"? (V. 2.)

_____ c. Why did Jesus heal the man who was "sick of the palsy"? (V. 6.)

_____ d. When Jesus saw Matthew, what did He say to him?

_____ e. What did Matthew do?

_____ f. How was the woman "diseased with an issue of blood" made whole? (V. 20.)

_____ g. How were the two blind men healed?

_____ h. What did Jesus do in the cities and villages?

_____ i. What did Jesus ask his disciples to do when he saw that the people "were scattered . . . , as sheep having no shepherd"? (V. 36.)

Matthew 10

_____ a. Who did Jesus call unto him?

_____ b. What power did Jesus give them?

_____ c. List the names of the twelve apostles Jesus called.

_____ d. List seven items of instruction that Jesus gave the Twelve Apostles in Matthew 10:5–16.

_____ e. Why would the disciples be brought before the rulers? (See also v. 18b, c.)

_____ f. Why were the disciples not to worry about what they should say to the rulers?

_____ g. Whom are we to fear?

_____ h. How are we to receive the Lord's apostles and prophets? Why?

Matthew 11

_____ a. What did Jesus say about John the Baptist?

_____ b. Who was the "Elias, which was for to come"? (Matthew 11:14; see v. 13a.)

_____ c. Why did Jesus upbraid the cities of Chorazin and Bethsaida?

_____ d. What is the promise for those who labor in the Lord's kingdom? (See also Mosiah 2:41.)

Matthew 12

_____ a. Why did the Pharisees complain to Jesus?

_____ b. What did Jesus say to them?

_____ c. How did Jesus respond to the question, "Is it lawful to heal on the sabbath days?" (Matthew 12:10.)

_____ d. How did Jesus respond to the charge of casting out devils in the name of Beelzebub? (See also v. 28c.)

_____ e. What sin will people not be forgiven of?

_____ f. How are we to be known?

_____ g. What will we account for in the day of judgment? (See also v. 36b, c.)

_____ h. Who seeks for a sign?

_____ i. What sign would be given to the people?

_____ j. Who are the brothers and sisters of Jesus? (See also Bible Dictionary, p. 627, s.v. "Brethren of the Lord.")

Matthew 13

_____ a. Why did Jesus speak to the people in parables? (See Matthew 13:12a; see also Bible Dictionary, p. 740, s.v. "Parables.")

Identify the following in the parable of the sower:

_____ b. What is the seed that is sown in the heart?

_____ c. Who received the seed by the wayside?

_____ d. Who received the seed in the stony places?

_____ e. Who received the seed among the thorns?

_____ f. Who received the seed in the good ground?

Identify the following in the parable of the wheat and the tares:

_____ g. Who sows the good seed?

_____ h. What is the field?

_____ i. Who are the good seed?

_____ j. Who are the tares?

_____ k. Who is the enemy that sowed the tares?

_____ l. Who are the reapers?

_____ m. What will happen at the end of the world? (See Matthew 13:39a.)

_____ n. Why is the kingdom of heaven like a net?

_____ o. What did the people of Jesus' own country say when he visited them?

_____ p. What did Jesus say to them?

_____ q. Why did Jesus not perform "many mighty works" in his own country? (V. 58.)

Matthew 14

_____ a. Why was Herod afraid to put John to death?

_____ b. Why was John finally beheaded?

_____ c. How many men were fed with the five loaves and two fishes?

_____ d. Why did Peter begin to sink while he was walking on the water to Jesus?

_____ e. How were the diseased healed?

Matthew 15

VERSE NUMBER

_____ a. What did Esaias prophecy concerning the scribes and Pharisees? (See also Isaiah 29:13.)

_____ b. What "defileth a man"? Why? (Matthew 15:11.)

_____ c. What did Jesus say would happen if "the blind lead the blind"? (V. 14.)

_____ d. Why was the woman's daughter made whole?

_____ e. Why did the multitude glorify the God of Israel?

_____ f. What did Jesus do for the multitude before leaving them? Why?

Matthew 16

VERSE NUMBER

_____ a. What did Jesus mean when he said, "Take heed and beware of the leaven of the Pharisees and of the Sadducees"? (Matthew 16:6.)

_____ b. Who did Peter say that Christ was?

_____ c. Why was Peter blessed? (See also Bible Dictionary, p. 749, s.v. "Peter.")

_____ d. What keys did Jesus promise to give Peter?

_____ e. What did Jesus begin to show his disciples?

_____ f. What must a man do who "take[s] up his cross"? (Matthew 16:24; see v. 24d.)

_____ g. What is required of us to save our soul? (See v. 25a.)

_____ h. How will every man be rewarded?

Matthew 17

_____ a. Who did Jesus take "up into an high mountain"? (Matthew 17:1.)

_____ b. How did Jesus appear to them?

_____ c. Who also appeared to the disciples?

_____ d. What did God the Father say to the disciples?

_____ e. What else was shown the disciples on the mount? (See D&C 63:20–21.)

_____ f. Who was the Elias that was prophesied to come? (See Matthew 17:11a.)

_____ g. Why could the disciples not cure the man's son?

_____ h. How did Jesus pay his taxes?

Matthew 18

_____ a. List two things we need to do to enter the kingdom of heaven.

_____ b. What did Jesus say about those who offend little children? (See Bible Dictionary, page 732, s.v. "Millstone.")

_____ c. What should we do when our brother trespasses against us?

_____ d. Why should we forgive one another?

Matthew 19

_____ a. Why did Moses allow divorce? (See also Bible Dictionary, p. 658, s.v. "Divorce.")

_____ b. What did Jesus tell the man to do to have eternal life?

_____ c. What did the young man do? Why?

_____ d. What will the Twelve Apostles do in the resurrection? (See also Matthew 19:28a; D&C 29:12.)

_____ e. How will those who follow Jesus be rewarded?

Matthew 20

_____ a. What did Jesus tell his disciples would happen to him at Jerusalem?

_____ b. What did Jesus say to those who wanted to be great?

_____ c. What did Jesus do for the two blind men?

Matthew 21

_____ a. How did Jesus enter Jerusalem? (See also Matthew 21:7a.)

_____ b. What did Jesus do to those who did evil in the temple? Why?

_____ c. What were the children doing in the temple?

_____ d. What did Jesus promise his disciples if they had faith?

_____ e. Why would the publicans and harlots go into the kingdom of God before the chief priests and elders? (See also v. 32d.)

_____ f. Why would the kingdom of God be given to another nation? (See v. 45a.)

Matthew 22

_____ a. How did Jesus answer the question "Is it lawful to give tribute unto Caesar, or not?" (Matthew 22:17.)

_____ b. What is the greatest commandment?

_____ c. What is the second greatest commandment?

Matthew 23

_____ a. Why were the people to be aware of the works of the scribes and the Pharisees?

_____ b. For what reason do the scribes and the Pharisees do their works?

_____ c. What does the word *Rabbi* mean? (See Matthew 23:7*a*.)

_____ d. What did the scribes and Pharisees omit in performing their religious obligations?

_____ e. How does verse 28 describe the scribes and Pharisees? (See also v. 24*a*.)

_____ f. Why were the current leaders more guilty than their fathers? (See v. 36*a*.)

Matthew 24

See also Questions on Joseph Smith–Matthew in this guide.

_____ a. What did Jesus say to his disciples about the last days?

_____ b. Why will the disciples "be hated of all nations"? (Matthew 24:9.)

_____ c. Who will deceive many?

_____ d. Why will "the love of many . . . wax cold"? (V. 12.)

_____ e. What will happen before the end comes?

_____ f. How great were the tribulations to be at the time of the destruction of Jerusalem in A.D. 70?

_____ g. Who will show great signs and wonders?

_____ h. What will happen "immediately after the tribulation of those days"? (V. 29.)

_____ i. How will Jesus appear at the Second Coming?

_____ j. What will people be doing when Jesus comes again?

_____ k. Why should we live as though Jesus were coming today?

Matthew 25

VERSE NUMBER

_____ a. What is the oil in the lamps? (See Matthew 25:1*b*.)

_____ b. What did the foolish virgins fail to do?

_____ c. What did the wise virgins do?

_____ d. Why are we always to be ready for the Second Coming?

_____ e. What did the servant who was given five talents do with them?

_____ f. How did the lord of the servants reward him?

_____ g. What did he who was given one talent do with it?

_____ h. How did the lord of the servants reward him?

_____ i. Who will be on the right hand of the Lord? On the left?

_____ j. When did the righteous feed and clothe the Lord?

_____ k. What will happen to the wicked who are on the left hand of the Lord?

Matthew 26

_____ a. What did "the chief priests, and the scribes, and the elders of the people" seek to do to Jesus? (Matthew 26:3.)

_____ b. What did Judas conspire to do?

_____ c. What did Jesus say at the Last Supper about being betrayed?

_____ d. Why were the disciples to eat the bread? (See v. 26b.)

_____ e. Why were the disciples to drink the wine? (See v. 28a.)

_____ f. What did the disciples do just before going to the Mount of Olives?

_____ g. In his prayer to his Father, what did Jesus promise to do?

_____ h. Why did Peter fall asleep?

_____ i. What did the disciples do when Jesus was taken away?

_____ j. How did the leaders seek to have cause to put Jesus to death?

_____ k. For what cause were they going to put Jesus to death?

_____ l. Why did Peter go out and weep bitterly?

Matthew 27

_____ a. What did the chief priests and elders do with Jesus in the morning?

_____ b. What did Judas do? (See also Matthew 27:5a.)

_____ c. What message did the wife of Pilate give to her husband?

_____ d. Why did the people want Barrabas released?

_____ e. What did Pilate do and say? (See also Bible Dictionary, p. 751, s.v. "Pilate.")

_____ f. What did the people reply?

_____ g. What did the soldiers do to Jesus before crucifying him?

_____ h. What did the Jews say to Jesus as he was upon the cross?

_____ i. What did Jesus say when he cried "with a loud voice"? (Matthew 27:50; see v. 50a.)

_____ j. List four things that happened at Jesus' death or soon after. (See also 3 Nephi 8–10.)

_____ k. What happened to the body of Jesus?

_____ l. Why was the tomb sealed up and guarded? (See also Matthew 27:64a.)

Matthew 28

VERSE NUMBER

_____ a. Who moved the stone that sealed the tomb? (See Matthew 28:2a.)

_____ b. What did the angels say to the women? (See also v. 5a.)

_____ c. What did the women do when they met Jesus?

_____ d. What did the chief priests and elders say to the soldiers?

_____ e. What did Jesus command the eleven disciples to do?

The Gospel According to St Mark

Introduction

See Bible Dictionary, p. 728, s.v. "Mark."

_____ a. By what name was Mark also called?

_____ b. Mark's gospel may have been written under whose direction?

_____ c. What is the purpose of Mark's writing?

_____ d. According to tradition, what did Mark do after Peter's death?

Mark 1

VERSE NUMBER

_____ a. How did Joseph Smith entitle the book of Mark? (See footnote to the title, p. 1241.)

_____ b. What did John the Baptist do? (See also Bible Dictionary, p. 618, s.v. "Baptism.")

_____ c. What happened when Jesus "was baptized of John"? (Mark 1:9.)

_____ d. What did the Spirit do? (See v. 12a.)

_____ e. Who ministered to Jesus in the wilderness?

_____ f. What did Jesus say to Simon and Andrew?

_____ g. What did they do?

_____ h. What did James and John do when Jesus called them? (See also Bible Dictionary, p. 715, s.v. "John.")

_____ i. What did Jesus do for those who came to him?

_____ j. What did Jesus do for the man who had leprosy?

Mark 2

VERSE NUMBER

_____ a. How did Jesus teach the people that he had power to forgive sin?

_____ b. Who sat with Jesus when he ate?

_____ c. Why did Jesus say that he ate with such individuals?

_____ d. Why was the Sabbath made? (See Mark 2:27b; also Bible Dictionary, p. 764, s.v. "Sabbath.")

Mark 3

VERSE NUMBER

_____ a. What principle of the gospel did Jesus try to teach the people about the Sabbath day?

20

_____ b. What was the reaction of the Pharisees to Jesus' healing on the Sabbath? (See also Bible Dictionary, p. 750, s.v. "Pharisees.")

_____ c. What did Jesus do for those who were afflicted?

_____ d. What did he ordain twelve disciples to do?

_____ e. What did Jesus say to those who accused him of casting out devils by the power of Satan?

_____ f. For what sin is there no forgiveness? (See also Mark 3:28a.)

Mark 4

VERSE NUMBER

_____ a. In the parable of the sower, what does the sower sow?

_____ b. What happened to those who were by the wayside?

_____ c. What happened to those who were on stony ground?

_____ d. What happened to those who were among thorns?

_____ e. What happened to those who were on good ground?

_____ f. Why should we keep all the commandments? (See also Mark 4:25a.)

_____ g. How is the kingdom of God like a grain of mustard seed? (See also Bible Dictionary, p. 736, s.v. "Mustard.")

_____ h. How did the disciples react when Jesus rebuked the wind?

Mark 5

VERSE NUMBER

_____ a. How did the unclean spirit in the man address Jesus?

_____ b. How many swine ran into the sea?

_____ c. What did Jesus say to him who had been possessed?

_____ d. How was the woman cured of the issue of blood?

_____ e. Who went with Jesus to the house of Jarius?

_____ f. How did Jesus raise the damsel?

Mark 6

VERSE NUMBER

_____ a. How did the people in Jesus' own country react when Jesus taught them?

_____ b. How many brothers did Jesus have? What were their names?

_____ c. How was the Savior restricted because of the unbelief of the people?

_____ d. How were members of the Quorum of Twelve Apostles to travel?

_____ e. What procedure did the Twelve use to heal the sick?

_____ f. How did Herod receive John the Baptist? (See also Mark 6:20b.)

_____ g. Why was John beheaded?

_____ h. Why did Jesus feed the five thousand?

_____ i. What did the people do as Jesus entered their villages? What was the result?

Mark 7

VERSE NUMBER

_____ a. What fault did the Pharisees find with the disciples?

_____ b. How did Jesus respond to their complaint?

_____ c. What law were the Pharisees not obeying?

_____ d. Explain Mark 7:15. (See also v. 15a, b.)

_____ e. Why would Jesus not prevent people from coming to him? (See v. 24a; also Map 16.)

_____ f. How did Jesus heal the man who was deaf?

Mark 8

VERSE NUMBER

_____ a. Why did Jesus feed the four thousand?

_____ b. What is the leaven of the Pharisees? (See Matthew 16:12.)

_____ c. How did Jesus cure the blind man?

_____ d. Whom did Peter say Jesus was?

_____ e. What did Jesus begin to teach them?

_____ f. Who will be clothed with glory and stand on the right hand of the Son of God? (See Mark 8:38c.)

Mark 9

_____ a. Who did Jesus take to a high mountain?

_____ b. How did Jesus appear to them on the mount?

_____ c. Who also appeared to them on the mount? (See Mark 9:4a.)

_____ d. What did God the Father say to the three apostles?

_____ e. Why were the disciples unable to cast out the evil spirit?

_____ f. What had the disciples disputed about among themselves?

_____ g. What callenge did Jesus give them because of their contention?

_____ h. Whom should we be careful not to offend?

Mark 10

_____ a. Why did Moses allow divorce?

_____ b. What did Jesus say about divorce?

_____ c. What did Jesus say when the little children came to see him?

_____ d. What did Jesus do for the children?

_____ e. What challenge did Jesus give the rich man who wanted eternal life?

_____ f. What must a person be willing to do to be saved in the kingdom of God? (See Mark 10:27a.)

_____ g. What did Jesus teach the Twelve on the way to Jerusalem?

_____ h. What is the greatest among them to do? Why?

_____ i. How was the blind man healed?

Mark 11

_____ a. What did the people say as Jesus entered Jerusalem? (See also Mark 11:10a.)

_____ b. What did Jesus do in the temple? Why? (See also Map 17.)

_____ c. Why did the scribes and Pharisees seek to destroy Jesus?

_____ d. List two things we should do when we pray.

_____ e. What question did the chief priests, the scribes, and the elders ask Jesus?

_____ f. How did Jesus confound them?

Mark 12

_____ a. Who were the wicked husbandmen in the parable?

_____ b. Why did they not "lay hold on" Jesus? (Mark 12:12.)

_____ c. How did Jesus answer the question "Is it lawful to give tribute to Caesar or not?" (V. 14.)

_____ d. Why is Jesus the God of the living? (See v. 27a.)

_____ e. Of all the commandments, which is the first, or greatest?

_____ f. Which commandment ranks second?

_____ g. Who will receive the greater damnation? Why?

_____ h. Why did the Savior say that the poor widow cast more into the treasury than did all the rich?

Mark 13

_____ a. List nine events that will precede the Second Coming.

_____ b. What will Jesus send his angels to do when he comes in glory?

_____ c. Who knows when the Second Coming will be? (See also Joseph Smith—Matthew 1:40.)

_____ d. Why should we be doing our duty and watching always?

Mark 14

_____ a. What did the chief priests and scribes seek to do?

_____ b. Why did they not take Jesus on the feast day?

_____ c. Why did the woman come and anoint Jesus? (See also Mark 14:8a.)

_____ d. What did Judas Iscariot do?

_____ e. Why were the disciples to eat the bread and drink the wine? (See v. 22a.)

_____ f. What did Jesus say that Peter would do that very night?

_____ g. What did the disciples do in their hearts while they were on their way to Gethsemane? (See v. 32a.)

_____ h. What did Jesus say to Peter, James, and John? (See v. 32a.)

_____ i. What did Jesus pray to his Father?

_____ j. How did Judas betray Jesus?

_____ k. Where was Jesus taken?

_____ l. What problem was caused with having false witnesses?

_____ m. How did Jesus answer the high priest?

_____ n. How did they treat Jesus?

_____ o. What did Peter do after denying Jesus three times?

Mark 15

_____ a. What did the chief priests do in the morning?

_____ b. How did Jesus respond to Pilate? (See also Mark 15:2b.)

_____ c. Why had the chief priests delivered Jesus to Pilate?

_____ d. Why were the people against Jesus?

_____ e. What did the soldiers do to Jesus?

_____ f. How did Satan tempt Jesus while he was on the cross?

_____ g. What did Jesus cry at the ninth hour of the day?

_____ h. What happened when Jesus died?

_____ i. Who was watching Jesus from a distance?

_____ j. What did Joseph of Arimathaea do? (See also v. 43b.)

Mark 16

_____ a. Who came to the sepulchre Sunday morning? Why? (See also Bible Dictionary, p. 627, s.v. "Burial.")

_____ b. What did the angels in the tomb say to them? (See Mark 16:4a.)

_____ c. Who did Jesus appear to first?

_____ d. What commandment did Jesus give to the Quorum of the Twelve Apostles?

_____ e. What signs will "follow them that believe"? (V. 17.)

_____ f. What did the disciples do after the Lord was taken up to heaven?

The Gospel According to St Luke

Introduction

See Bible Dictionary, page 726, s.v. "Luke."

_____ a. What was Luke's profession?

_____ b. What is our first information about him?

_____ c. Who did Luke direct his testimony to?

Luke 1

_____ a. How did Joseph Smith entitle the book of Luke? (See footnote to the title, p. 1271.)

_____ b. What was Luke's calling? (See Luke 1:1*a*.)

_____ c. What had many followers done?

_____ d. What did Luke have a "perfect understanding of"? (V. 3.)

_____ e. What does the name *Theophilus* mean? (See Bible Dictionary, p. 785, s.v. "Theophilus.")

_____ f. How did Zacharias respond when he first saw the angel?

_____ g. What had Zacharias prayed for?

_____ h. What did the angel say to Zacharias?

_____ i. Who was the angel that appeared to Zacharias? (See Bible Dictionary, p. 676, s.v. "Gabriel.")

_____ j. What sign did Gabriel give Zacharias? Why?

_____ k. Who visited Mary? (See also Bible Dictionary, p. 729, s.v. "Mary.")

_____ l. What did the angel say to Mary?

_____ m. How did Mary respond?

_____ n. What did Mary say to Elisabeth?

_____ o. What did Zacharias prophesy about his son, John?

_____ p. What does Luke record about John's youth?

Luke 2

_____ a. Why did Joseph and Mary go to Bethlehem?

_____ b. What caused the shepherds to be afraid?

_____ c. What did the angel say to them?

_____ d. What did the shepherds do after the angels left?

_____ e. What did Simeon do when he saw Jesus?

_____ f. What did Luke record concerning Jesus' youth?

_____ g. What was Jesus doing when Joseph and Mary found him in the temple? (See Luke 2:46c.)

Luke 3

_____ a. What did John do in "all the country about Jordan"? (Luke 3:3.)

_____ b. List seven things Luke alludes to about the mission of Jesus. (See v. 4a.)

_____ c. What is the fate of every tree, or person, that "bringeth not forth good fruit"? (V. 9.)

_____ d. How did John testify of Jesus?

_____ e. What did Herod do to John? Why? (See also Bible Dictionary, p. 702, s.v. "Herodias.")

_____ f. Who bore witness of Jesus' being the Son of God at his baptism? (See also Bible Dictionary, p. 658, s.v. "Dove, Sign of"; p. 681, s.v. "God"; p. 704, s.v. "Holy Ghost.")

_____ g. About how old was Jesus when he was baptized?

Luke 4

_____ a. Where did the Spirit of God lead Jesus after his baptism?

_____ b. How long did Jesus fast?

_____ c. List the three temptations, which Jesus resisted.

_____ d. What did those in the synagogue at Nazareth seek to do to Jesus? (See also Map 15.)

_____ e. How did Jesus escape?

_____ f. Who obeyed Jesus because he had authority and power?

_____ g. What did Jesus do for the sick who were brought to him?

_____ h. Where did Jesus preach the gospel?

Luke 5

_____ a. What did Jesus ask Simon Peter to do? (See also Luke 5:4a.)

_____ b. What happened as a result of Simon's obedience?

_____ c. What did the Lord say to Peter? (See also v. 10a.)

_____ d. What did Jesus do for the leper?

_____ e. Why did great multitudes come to Jesus?

_____ f. What did Jesus say to the man with palsy? (See also v. 18a.)

_____ g. What did Jesus say to those who complained that he ate with publicans and sinners?

Luke 6

_____ a. What did Jesus ask the scribes and Pharisees before healing the man with a withered hand? Why?

_____ b. What was the reaction of the scribes and Pharisees to the miracle?

_____ c. What did Jesus do in preparation for choosing the Quorum of the Twelve Apostles?

_____ d. What did Jesus call the twelve disciples whom he had chosen? (See also Bible Dictionary, p. 612, s.v. "Apostle.")

_____ e. Why did a great multitude of people come to Jesus?

_____ f. Who did Jesus say would be blessed?

_____ g. In Luke 6:27–38, what did Jesus instruct his disciples to do?

_____ h. What is the promise for those who give?

_____ i. What happens when the blind lead the blind? (See also v. 39c.)

_____ j. What should we do instead of criticizing others?

_____ k. How can we discern good people from bad people?

_____ l. Who is like the person who built his foundation on a rock?

_____ m. Who is like the person who built his foundation on the earth?

Luke 7

_____ a. What did Jesus say to those who followed him when he received the centurion's message?

_____ b. What did Jesus do for the widow in the city of Nain?

_____ c. Who will be blessed?

_____ d. What did Jesus say of John?

_____ e. Why did the Lord forgive the woman of her sins?

Luke 8

_____ a. What did Jesus do "throughout every city and village"? (Luke 8:1.)

_____ b. Who was healed of evil spirits?

_____ c. In the parable of the sower, what is the seed?

_____ d. Who are they by the wayside?

_____ e. Who are they on the rock?

_____ f. Who are they among thorns?

_____ g. Who are they on good ground?

_____ h. What did his disciples say to one another when Jesus rebuked the wind?

_____ i. What did the evil spirit say to Jesus?

_____ j. How did Jesus know that someone had touched him?

_____ k. What did Jesus say to the woman?

_____ l. What did Jesus do for the twelve-year-old daughter of Jairus?

Luke 9

_____ a. What power and authority did Jesus give to his twelve disciples?

_____ b. What did he send them to do?

_____ c. What did he instruct them to do?

_____ d. What did Jesus do for those who followed him?

_____ e. What did Jesus say would happen to him?

_____ f. What must we be willing to do to save our lives? Why? (See Luke 9:24a.)

_____ g. Who did Jesus speak with on the mountain?

_____ h. What did they speak about? (See v. 31a.)

Luke 10

_____ a. Who did Jesus send "into every city and place" to prepare his way? (Luke 10:1.)

_____ b. What were they to say upon entering a house?

_____ c. What were they to do in that house?

_____ d. What did the seventy say to the Lord when they returned?

_____ e. What power did Jesus give them?

_____ f. Why were they to rejoice?

_____ g. How are we to love the Lord to obtain eternal life?

_____ h. Who is our neighbor?

Luke 11

_____ a. What did the disciples ask Jesus to teach them?

_____ b. What do we need to do before asking our Father in Heaven to forgive us?

_____ c. What will our Heavenly Father do for us when we are in need? (See also Luke 11:5a.)

_____ d. What is our position if we are not for the Lord?

_____ e. Why was the Savior's generation an evil generation?

_____ f. Where is the light of the body?

_____ g. What will happen if the eye is single to God?

_____ h. What did the Lord tell the Pharisees? (See v. 41a.)

_____ i. Whose blood would "be required of this generation"? (V. 50.)

_____ j. Why were the lawyers cursed? (See v. 52c.)

_____ k. Why did the scribes and Pharisees seek to provoke Jesus?

Luke 12

_____ a. What will happen to those who seek to hide their evil deeds?

_____ b. Who are we to fear?

_____ c. Who will "the Son of man also confess before the angels of God"? (Luke 12:8; see also v. 9a.)

_____ d. Who will teach the missionaries what to say when they are questioned?

_____ e. Why should we not seek to lay up great material treasures?

_____ f. What should we seek first? (See v. 31a.)

_____ g. Where will our heart, or interest, be?

_____ h. Which servants will be blessed when the Lord comes? (See also v. 38a.)

_____ i. What will happen to those who know the Lord's will but do not prepare for his coming or keep the commandments?

Luke 13

VERSE NUMBER

_____ a. What is required of us if we are to avoid perishing?

_____ b. What did the Lord do for the infirm woman?

_____ c. Why did Jesus rebuke the ruler of the synagogue?

_____ d. What was the reaction of the people after Jesus rebuked the leader of the synagogue?

_____ e. When would there be "weeping and gnashing of teeth"? (Luke 13:28.)

_____ f. Why could the Lord not save Jerusalem?

Luke 14

VERSE NUMBER

_____ a. How did Jesus answer those who criticized him for healing on the sabbath?

_____ b. What will happen to "whosoever exalteth himself"? (Luke 14:11.)

_____ c. Why should we help the poor?

_____ d. What is the Lord referring to in verses 28 through 30? (See v. 30a.)

Luke 15

VERSE NUMBER

_____ a. In the parable of the lost sheep, who are the lost sheep?

_____ b. In the parable of the piece of silver, what does the piece of silver represent?

_____ c. In the parable of the prodigal son, why did the father prepare the feast?

Luke 16

VERSE NUMBER

_____ a. How should we respond when the Lord asks us to do little things? Why?

_____ b. Why can we not serve both God and the world?

_____ c. What did the rich man desire of Abraham?

_____ d. What did Abraham reply?

Luke 17

VERSE NUMBER

_____ a. What would be better to happen to someone "than that he should offend one of these little ones"?

_____ b. What should we do when someone offends us? (See Luke 17:3a.)

_____ c. What did the apostles ask of the Lord?

_____ d. How many of the ten lepers returned to thank Jesus for cleansing them?

_____ e. What is the second coming of the Lord to be like?

_____ f. What will be happening when Jesus comes again?

_____ g. What warning is found in verses 34 through 37? (See v. 37a.)

Luke 18

VERSE NUMBER

_____ a. Why did the unjust judge agree to help the widow?

_____ b. How does the parable of the unjust judge relate to God as judge? (See also Luke 18:8a.)

_____ c. Why was the publican justified in his prayer?

_____ d. How should we receive the kingdom of God?

_____ e. Why was the ruler who wanted to follow Jesus sorrowful?

_____ f. What is required of us to enter the kingdom of God? (See v. 27a.)

_____ g. What did Jesus say would happen to him in Jerusalem?

_____ h. What did the people do when Jesus healed the blind man?

Luke 19

_____ a. How did Zacchaeus receive Jesus?

_____ b. How does the parable of the pounds relate to us? (See also Luke 19:26a.)

_____ c. Why did the multitude praise God as Jesus entered Jerusalem?

_____ d. What did Jesus say as he came near Jerusalem?

_____ e. How did the people accept Jesus?

Luke 20

_____ a. What question did Jesus ask the chief priests who wanted to know where he got his authority?

_____ b. Why were they afraid to answer?

_____ c. What did the owner of the vineyard do to the wicked husbandman? Why?

_____ d. How did the chief priests seek to destroy Jesus?

_____ e. Who did Jesus tell the people to beware of?

Luke 21

See also Questions on Joseph Smith—Matthew in this guide.

_____ a. How had the poor woman donated more than all the rich?

_____ b. What did Jesus warn the people against?

_____ c. List six signs that will precede the destruction of Jerusalem. (See also Luke 21:24f.)

_____ d. List four signs that will precede the Second Coming. (See v. 25a.)

_____ e. What must we do "to stand before the Son of man" ? (V. 36; see also v. 36c.)

_____ f. What did the people do early the next morning? Why?

Luke 22

_____ a. What did the chief priests and scribes seek to do?

_____ b. What agreement did Judas make with the chief priests?

_____ c. Why were the apostles instructed to eat the bread and drink the wine?

_____ d. What is required of those who seek to be great?

_____ e. What was Simon Peter instructed to do when he was converted?

_____ f. What did the apostles lack when preaching the gospel?

_____ g. What did Jesus commit to do in his prayer to his Father?

_____ h. Who strengthened Jesus as he prayed?

_____ i. Why did Peter weep bitterly?

_____ j. What did the guards do to Jesus that night?

_____ k. Where did they take Jesus the next morning?

Luke 23

_____ a. What did Pilate ask Jesus?

_____ b. Why did Pilate order Jesus to be crucified? (See also Bible Dictionary, p. 651, s.v. "Crucifixion.")

_____ c. What did Jesus say about those who crucified him? (See also Luke 23:34c.)

_____ d. What did Jesus say just before he died?

_____ e. What did Joseph of Arimathaea do? (See also v. 50a.)

Luke 24

_____ a. What did those who came to care for the body of Jesus find when they reached the sepulcher? (See also Luke 24:2a.)

_____ b. What did the two angels tell them?

_____ c. What did Peter do upon hearing the women's story?

_____ d. What did Cleopas say to Jesus as they traveled to Emmaus?

_____ e. When were the disciples' eyes opened?

_____ f. What did the two disciples say to each other when Jesus disappeared?

_____ g. What did Jesus say when he first appeared to his disciples in Jerusalem?

_____ h. What did Jesus do to help them understand the nature of a resurrected being?

_____ i. What did Jesus tell them before he left them?

_____ j. What did the apostles do after Jesus ascended into heaven?

The Gospel According to St John

Introduction

See Bible Dictionary, page 715, s.v. "John, Gospel of."

_____ a. What is the object of John's writing?

_____ b. What was Christ's status in the premortal existence?

_____ c. What does John emphasize in his testimony?

_____ d. How is John's gospel different from the other three?

John 1

_____ a. How did Joseph Smith entitle the book of John? (See footnote to the title, p. 1324.)

_____ b. What title did Jesus have in the premortal earth life? (See John 1:1a.)

_____ c. What was the mission of John? (See v. 1a.)

_____ d. What is the light that "lighteth every man that cometh into the world"? (v. 9; see v. 1a; see also Bible Dictionary, p. 725, s.v. "Light of Christ.")

_____ e. Why is this light given to every man? (See Moroni 7:16.)

_____ f. Who did John the Baptist say that he was?

_____ g. What did John the Baptist say to the people when he saw Jesus?

_____ h. What did Andrew say to Simon Peter about Jesus?

_____ i. What did Philip say to Nathanael about Jesus?

_____ j. What did Jesus say that Nathanael would see?

John 2

VERSE NUMBER

_____ a. What did Jesus say to his mother when she told him there was no more wine? (See John 2:4a.)

_____ b. What was the first miracle Jesus performed in Cana of Galilee?

_____ c. What did Jesus do in the temple? Why?

_____ d. What temple did Jesus refer to when he said he would raise it up in three days?

John 3

VERSE NUMBER

_____ a. Who was Nicodemus?

_____ b. How did Jesus answer Nicodemus in John 3:5?

_____ c. What was the testimony of Jesus that was given to the Sanhedrin? (See v. 11b.)

_____ d. How do we know that God loves his children?

_____ e. Why do people love darkness rather than light?

_____ f. What will people receive who believe in the Son? (See v. 36a.)

John 4

_____ a. Why did the Pharisees seek Jesus' life? (See John 4:1a.)

_____ b. What did Jesus offer to give the woman?

_____ c. How are we to worship God? (See also v. 24a.)

_____ d. Who did Jesus tell the woman he was? (See also v. 26a.)

_____ e. What did the woman do when the disciples came?

_____ f. How was Jesus received by the Samaritans? (See Bible Dictionary, p. 768, s.v. "Samaritans.")

_____ g. What was the second miracle Jesus did in Cana? (See v. 54.)

John 5

_____ a. Why did the Jews persecute Jesus and seek to slay him?

_____ b. In which verses does Jesus testify that he will visit the dead after his crucifixion?

_____ c. Who has borne witness of Jesus? (See also John 5:32a.)

_____ d. What written testimony do we have that Jesus is the Son of God?

John 6

_____ a. Why did the great multitude follow Jesus?

_____ b. What did the men say who saw the miracle of the feeding of the five thousand?

_____ c. Why did Jesus depart from the multitude?

_____ d. Why did the people follow Jesus? (See also John 6:26a.)

_____ e. Why did Jesus come to the earth?

_____ f. What is the Father's will? (See also v. 40c.)

_____ g. Who will the Lord raise up in the resurrection of the just? (See v. 44a.)

_____ h. Why did the Twelve Apostles stay with Jesus? (See also v. 69a.)

John 7

VERSE NUMBER

_____ a. Why does the world hate Jesus?

_____ b. How may we know the truth of the doctrine taught by Jesus?

_____ c. What did the people think of Christ?

John 8

VERSE NUMBER

_____ a. What was the penalty for adultery under the law of Moses?

_____ b. What did Jesus say to the scribes and Pharisees?

_____ c. What did Jesus say to the woman?

_____ d. Why is the Father always with Jesus?

_____ e. What did Jesus promise those who believed in him?

_____ f. When are we not free?

_____ g. How were the Jews different from Abraham?

_____ h. How did Jesus describe the devil?

_____ i. Why should we receive the words of God? (See John 8:47a.)

_____ j. How did the Jews react to Jesus when he declared himself to be I Am? (See also v. 58b.)

John 9

VERSE NUMBER

_____ a. Why was it important for Jesus to do the works of the Father "while it is day"? (John 9:4; see also v. 4c.)

_____ b. Why was there a division among the Pharisees?

_____ c. What did the parents of the blind man say to the Pharisees? Why?

_____ d. What did the blind man say to the Pharisees? (See also v. 32a; Bible Dictionary, p. 626, s.v. "Blindness.")

_____ e. What did the Pharisees do to the blind man?

_____ f. What did the blind man say to Jesus?

John 10

VERSE NUMBER

_____ a. Why do the sheep follow their shepherd? (See also Bible Dictionary, p. 773, s.v. "Sheep.")

_____ b. Why had the good shepherd come?

_____ c. Who were some of the other sheep that must hear the Lord's voice? (See 3 Nephi 15:11–24.)

_____ d. What was the Lord commanded by the Father to do?

_____ e. What did Jesus ask the Pharisees to do if they did not believe him?

John 11

VERSE NUMBER

_____ a. How did Jesus feel toward Mary, Martha, and Lazarus? (See also John 11:2a.)

_____ b. Why did the disciples fear the Jews? (See v. 16a.)

_____ c. How long had Lazarus been in the grave? (See also v. 17a.)

_____ d. Who did Jesus say that he was?

_____ e. Who did Martha believe that Jesus was?

_____ f. What did Jesus do when he saw Mary weeping?

_____ g. What happened when Jesus called Lazarus to come forth?

_____ h. Why did Jesus not go openly among the Jews?

John 12

_____ a. Why did Judas complain of Mary's use of the ointment? (See also John 12:6b.)

_____ b. What did Jesus tell Judas? (See v. 7a.)

_____ c. Why did the chief priests also want to kill Lazarus?

_____ d. When did the disciples understand much of what was done?

_____ e. What did the voice of the Father bear record of?

_____ f. What reason did Jesus give for that testimony?

_____ g. Why did many of the chief rulers who believed Jesus was the Son of God fail to confess or acknowledge it?

_____ h. Whose message did Jesus deliver to the people?

John 13

_____ a. What did Jesus do for his disciples after their supper?

_____ b. Why did Jesus wash their feet? (See John 13:8a.)

_____ c. Who are the people receiving when they receive the missionaries? (See also v. 20a.)

_____ d. What did Jesus say to Judas after He had given him the sop?

_____ e. What new commandment did Jesus give his disciples?

_____ f. How may all people know a true disciple of Christ?

John 14

_____ a. What did Jesus promise the disciples?

_____ b. What is the only way to come to the Father?

_____ c. What will people do who believe in Jesus?

_____ d. How can we know who loves God?

_____ e. What would the Father give to the disciples when Jesus left? (See headnote; Bible Dictionary, p. 648, s.v. "Comforter.")

_____ f. Why can't the world receive the Spirit of truth?

_____ g. What will Jesus do for those who keep his commandments? (See also John 14:21c.)

_____ h. What is part of the mission of the Holy Ghost?

_____ i. What did Jesus leave with his disciples?

John 15

_____ a. Why should we do the will of Jesus?

_____ b. How is the Father glorified?

_____ c. How are we to love one another?

_____ d. What is the greatest sacrifice a person can make for those whom he loves?

_____ e. What did Jesus call his disciples? Why?

_____ f. Why had the Lord chosen and ordained them?

_____ g. Why does the world hate the disciples?

_____ h. Why were the Jews under condemnation?

_____ i. Who would bear witness of Jesus?

John 16

_____ a. What would those who killed the apostles think? Why?

_____ b. Why did Jesus need to go away?

_____ c. What will the Holy Ghost do for the apostles when he comes?

_____ d. Who are we to ask for help?

_____ e. Why does the Father love the disciples?

_____ f. Why did Jesus tell the apostles these things?

John 17

VERSE NUMBER

_____ a. What must we do to have eternal life?

_____ b. What did Jesus report to his Father?

_____ c. How are Jesus and the Father one? (See John 17:11*b*.)

_____ d. List four things Jesus asked his Father to do.

John 18

VERSE NUMBER

_____ a. How did Judas know where to find Jesus?

_____ b. What did the mob do when Jesus said who he was?

_____ c. Where did the band of men take Jesus?

_____ d. What did Jesus say after being struck by one of the officers?

_____ e. Why could the Jews not put Jesus to death?

_____ f. What did Pilate say to the Jews after questioning Jesus?

John 19

VERSE NUMBER

_____ a. What did the chief priests and officers cry out when they saw Jesus?

_____ b. What did Pilate seek to do with Jesus?

_____ c. Whom did Jesus ask to care for his mother? (See headnote.)

_____ d. How was the scripture quoted in John 19:36 fulfilled?

_____ e. What did Nicodemus do? (See also v. 39a.)

John 20

_____ a. Who did Mary see at the tomb? (See John 20:1d.)

_____ b. Who went with Peter to the tomb of Jesus? (See headnote.)

_____ c. Why did Mary weep?

_____ d. What did Jesus say to Mary?

_____ e. Why was Mary not to touch Jesus?

_____ f. What did Jesus say to his disciples when he appeared to them?

_____ g. Who did he tell them to receive?

_____ h. What power did the apostles have?

_____ i. What did Jesus ask Thomas to do because of his doubts?

_____ j. Why were these things written?

John 21

_____ a. What were the apostles doing when Jesus called to them?

_____ b. What happened when they "cast the net on the right side of the ship"? (John 21:6.)

_____ c. What did Jesus ask them to do when they had come to shore?

_____ d. What did Jesus instruct Peter to do?

_____ e. What was to happen to John? (See D&C 7:3–4.)

The Acts of the Apostles

Introduction

See Bible Dictionary, page 603, s.v. "Acts of the Apostles."

_____ a. Who was the book of Acts written to?

_____ b. What is recorded in the first part of Acts? (See also Map 18.)

_____ c. What is outlined in the last half of Acts?

_____ d. List three places where the apostles were witnesses of Jesus.

_____ e. Whose preaching is recorded in the book of Acts?

Acts 1

VERSE NUMBER

_____ a. Who is the author of the book of Acts? (See Acts 1:1b; also Bible Dictionary, p. 726, s.v. "Luke.")

_____ b. How long did Jesus teach the disciples after his resurrection?

_____ c. Why were the apostles to stay in Jerusalem?

_____ d. Where were the apostles to be witnesses of Jesus?

_____ e. What did the two angels say when Jesus was taken up to heaven?

_____ f. How many people had gathered in the upper room?

_____ g. How was Matthias chosen to be an apostle to replace Judas?

Acts 2

VERSE NUMBER

_____ a. What happened on the day of Pentecost?

_____ b. In Acts 2:36, what did Peter testify?

_____ c. What did Peter instruct the people to do?

_____ d. How many people were baptized?

_____ e. What did the apostles do?

_____ f. What did they do who believed the teachings of the apostles?

Acts 3

VERSE NUMBER

_____ a. What did Peter say to the lame man who was at the temple gate?

_____ b. What did Peter say in Acts 3:12 to the people who gathered because of the miracle?

_____ c. What did Peter tell them to do?

_____ d. What must happen before the Second Coming?

Acts 4

_____ a. Why were Peter and John taken away?

_____ b. How many believed their words?

_____ c. By what power did Peter respond to the council?

_____ d. In whose name was the lame man made whole?

_____ e. What is the only name given under heaven by which we are saved?

_____ f. What did the council say to Peter and John?

_____ g. What did Peter and John reply?

_____ h. What happened after they prayed?

_____ i. Why was there no one "among them that lacked"? (Acts 4:34.)

Acts 5

_____ a. What happened to Ananias and Sapphira? Why? (See also Bible Dictionary, p. 651, s.v. "Covenant.")

_____ b. Who were the people afraid to follow? (See Acts 5:13a.)

_____ c. What happened to the sick who came?

_____ d. What did the angel instruct the apostles to do after they were freed from prison?

_____ e. What did Peter and the other apostles say to the council?

_____ f. How did the members of the council respond?

_____ g. What did Gamaliel recommend be done? Why? (See also v. 39a.)

Acts 6

_____ a. What kind of men did the apostles seek after to help them?

_____ b. What was the result of calling these men?

_____ c. When disputing with Stephen, what were the men unable to resist?

_____ d. What did they do because they disagreed with Stephen?

_____ e. What did the council see when they looked at Stephen's face?

Acts 7

_____ a. How long were the children of Israel in bondage to the Egyptians?

_____ b. Why did the children of Israel move to Egypt?

_____ c. Why did Moses flee from Egypt?

_____ d. Why did Moses return to Egypt?

_____ e. What did the Jews do to the prophets who testified of Christ?

_____ f. Who did Stephen see as he looked into heaven?

_____ g. What did the council do to Stephen?

Acts 8

_____ a. What happened to the church in Jerusalem at the time of Stephen's death?

_____ b. What was Saul doing to the members of the Church?

_____ c. Why did Peter and John go to Samaria?

_____ d. What did Peter say to Simon when he offered the apostles money?

_____ e. What was Simon's response to Peter?

_____ f. What did the Spirit instruct Philip to do?

_____ g. Why was the eunuch baptized?

_____ h. What happened to Philip?

Acts 9

_____ a. Why was Saul going to Damascus?

_____ b. What did Jesus say to Saul?

_____ c. How long did Saul fast?

_____ d. What did Jesus instruct Ananias to do?

_____ e. What was the mission of Saul to be? (See also Bible Dictionary, p. 679, s.v. "Gentile.")

_____ f. What did Saul do in Damascus?

_____ g. Why were the disciples in Jerusalem afraid of Saul?

_____ h. What did Peter do for Tabitha?

Acts 10

_____ a. List five things we learn about Cornelius in Acts 10:1 and 2. (See also Bible Dictionary, p. 650, s.v. "Cornelius.")

_____ b. What did the angel tell Cornelius to do?

_____ c. What message did the servants of Cornelius deliver to Peter?

_____ d. Why did Peter go to Cornelius, who was a gentile?

_____ e. To whom did Jesus show himself after the resurrection?

_____ f. What did Peter command those gathered at the home of Cornelius to do?

Acts 11

VERSE NUMBER

_____ a. What explanation did Peter give the Jewish members of the Church for preaching to the gentiles?

_____ b. How was this explanation received?

_____ c. How long did Barnabas and Saul preach in Antioch?

_____ d. What were the members of the Church called in Antioch?

_____ e. What did the disciples do for their brethren in Judea? (See also Acts 11:28b.)

Acts 12

VERSE NUMBER

_____ a. What happened to James?

_____ b. What did the Church do when Peter was put in prison?

_____ c. How was Peter freed from prison?

_____ d. What happened to Herod? Why?

Acts 13

VERSE NUMBER

_____ a. How were Barnabas and Saul called into missionary service? (See also Map 19.)

_____ b. By what name was Saul now called? (See also Bible Dictionary, p. 742, s.v. "Paul.")

_____ c. What did Paul do to Elymas, the sorcerer?

_____ d. What did Paul testify of in the synagogue in Antioch?

_____ e. What did the gentiles say to Paul when he finished speaking?

_____ f. Who came to hear the word of God on the next sabbath?

_____ g. Why were Paul and Barnabas teaching the gentiles?

Acts 14

_____ a. What did Paul and Barnabas do in Iconium?

_____ b. What did the people do when Paul healed the crippled man?

_____ c. What did Paul say to them?

_____ d. Why was Paul stoned?

_____ e. What did they do when visiting the churches?

Acts 15

_____ a. What was the cause of the dissension?

_____ b. How was the conflict to be resolved?

_____ c. What had God done for the gentile? (See also Bible Dictionary, p. 650, s.v. "Conversion.")

_____ d. What did Paul and Barnabas declare to the council?

_____ e. What was the recommendation of James on the matter?

_____ f. What was the message of the apostles to those in Antioch?

_____ g. Why was there a contention between Paul and Barnabas?

Acts 16

_____ a. Why did Paul not go to Asia?

_____ b. Why did Paul go to Macedonia? (See also Map 20.)

_____ c. Who was Lydia?

_____ d. How did Paul cast out the "spirit of divination" that possessed the damsel?

_____ e. What did the magistrates do to Paul and Silas?

_____ f. What did the keeper of the prison do?

_____ g. Why did the magistrates fear?

Acts 17

_____ a. What was Paul's message to the Thessalonians?

_____ b. How was his message received?

_____ c. How was his message received in Berea?

_____ d. Who stirred up the people in Berea?

_____ e. What was the city of Athens like? (See also Acts 17:16a.)

_____ f. What did Paul say to the Athenians about the inscription on the altar?

_____ g. What did the Athenians do when Paul talked of the resurrection?

Acts 18

_____ a. Who did Paul stay with in Corinth? Why?

_____ b. What did Paul do on each sabbath?

_____ c. What did he testify to the Jews?

_____ d. What did Paul say to the Jews when they rejected his testimony?

_____ e. What did the Lord tell Paul in the night by a vision?

_____ f. How did Gallio deal with the accusations against Paul?

_____ g. What did Paul do in Ephesus?

_____ h. Who was Apollos?

_____ i. What did Apollos do after meeting Priscilla and Aquila?

Acts 19

_____ a. What did Paul do for the disciples in Ephesus? (See also Bible Dictionary, p. 665, s.v. "Ephesus.")

_____ b. What miracles did God perform through Paul?

_____ c. What happened to the sons of Sceva?

_____ d. What did many do, who had used sorcery? (See also Acts 19:19a.)

_____ e. Why did Demetrius and the other craftsmen stir up the people against the disciples? (See also Bible Dictionary, p. 657, s.v. "Diana.")

_____ f. What did the town clerk say to the people?

Acts 20

_____ a. Why did the disciples come together on the first day of the week? (See Acts 20:7a, d; also Map 21.)

_____ b. What happened to Eutychus?

_____ c. When did Paul finish speaking?

_____ d. What did the Holy Ghost witness to Paul about his future? (See also Acts 20:23b.)

_____ e. What was the attitude of Paul about his future?

_____ f. What were the final words of Paul to the disciples from Ephesus?

_____ g. Which verses in Paul's speech describe the apostasy that was to come?

Acts 21

_____ a. What did Paul do with the disciples from Tyre before leaving them?

_____ b. What did Agabus prophesy?

_____ c. What did the disciples do when they heard this prophecy?

_____ d. How did Paul respond to them?

_____ e. What did Paul report in Jerusalem about his ministry?

_____ f. Who stirred up the people against Paul?

_____ g. What prevented the Jews from killing Paul?

Acts 22

_____ a. What had Paul done before his conversion?

_____ b. How was Paul converted?

_____ c. Why did Jesus tell Paul to leave Jerusalem?

_____ d. To whom was Paul to preach the gospel?

_____ e. How was Paul's story received by his audience?

_____ f. Why was Paul not scourged? (See also Acts 22:29a.)

Acts 23

_____ a. What did Paul say to Ananias?

_____ b. What did the Sadducees deny? (See also Bible Dictionary, p. 761, s.v. "Resurrection.")

_____ c. What did the Pharisees believe?

_____ d. What did the chief captain command his soldiers to do? Why?

_____ e. What did the Lord say to Paul?

_____ f. What did forty of the Jews bind themselves under a curse to do?

_____ g. How was the plot made known to the chief captain?

_____ h. What did the chief captain do?

Acts 24

_____ a. Who came to speak against Paul?

_____ b. What was Paul accused of?

_____ c. What did Paul report in his defense? (See also Bible Dictionary, p. 649, s.v. "Conscience.")

_____ d. What did Felix command the centurion regarding Paul?

_____ e. What did Paul teach Felix and Drusilla? (See also Acts 24:25a.)

_____ f. Why did Felix leave Paul bound?

Acts 25

_____ a. What did the high priest do when Festus came to Jerusalem?

_____ b. What did the Jews do before Festus as he sat on the judgment seat in Caesarea?

_____ c. Why did Festus ask Paul to go to Jerusalem?

_____ d. What was Paul's reply? (See also Map 22.)

_____ e. Who came to visit Festus?

_____ f. Why did Festus desire to bring Paul before King Agrippa?

Acts 26

_____ a. Why was Paul pleased to stand before King Agrippa?

_____ b. What did Paul say of his youth?

_____ c. What did Paul do before his conversion?

_____ d. What did Paul say of his conversion?

_____ e. What was Paul called to do among the Gentiles? Why?

_____ f. Why did the Jews seek to kill Paul?

_____ g. What did Festus say to Paul?

_____ h. What did King Agrippa say to Paul?

_____ i. What did Paul reply to King Agrippa?

_____ j. What did King Agrippa say to Festus?

Acts 27

_____ a. What did Julius, a centurion, do for Paul at Sidon?

_____ b. What warning did Paul give to those on the ship?

_____ c. Why did the crew and passengers give up hope of being saved?

_____ d. What did Paul prophesy?

_____ e. Why did Paul encourage them to eat?

_____ f. How many people were on the ship?

_____ g. How were they all saved?

Acts 28

_____ a. How were the missionaries received by the barbarians?

_____ b. Why did the barbarians think Paul was a god?

_____ c. How did Paul bless those on the island?

_____ d. Why did Paul call "the chief of the Jews together"? (Acts 28:17.)

_____ e. What did Paul preach to them on the day appointed him?

_____ f. How was his message received?

_____ g. Who is the Old Testament prophet Paul quotes? Why?

_____ h. What did Paul do for two years in Rome?

The Epistles of Paul

Introduction

See Bible Dictionary, page 743, s.v. "Pauline Epistles."

_____ a. Who were Paul's epistles written to?

_____ b. In what order are they placed in the New Testament?

_____ c. What is the advantage of studying these epistles in chronological order?

_____ d. When were the epistles in each of the four groups written?

_____ e. What epistles make up the first group? Where were they written? (See Bible Dictionary, p. 743, s.v. "Pauline Epistles—The First Group.")

_____ f. What epistles make up the second group? Where were they written? (See Bible Dictionary, p. 743, s.v. "Pauline Epistles—The Second Group.")

_____ g. List three important characteristics of the second group.

_____ h. What epistles make up the third group? Where were they written? (See Bible Dictionary, p. 745, s.v. "Pauline Epistles—The Third Group.")

_____ i. List two important characteristics of the third group.

_____ j. What are the epistles in the fourth group called? (See Bible Dictionary, p. 747, s.v. "Pauline Epistles—The Fourth Group.")

_____ k. What do they deal with?

_____ l. What do we learn from them?

_____ m. To whom are the epistles of the fourth group addressed?

_____ n. What kind of question is discussed in these epistles?

_____ o. What has taken the place of instruction in the faith?

_____ p. What do we learn from Paul's writings? (See Bible Dictionary, p. 748, s.v. "Pauline Epistles—Summary.")

_____ q. What must we remember about these writings?

_____ r. What does the New Testament presuppose its readers know?

_____ s. How was Paul's life characterized?

_____ t. What is Paul's greatest contribution?

The Epistle of Paul the Apostle to the Romans

Introduction

See Bible Dictionary, page 745, s.v. "Pauline Epistles—Epistle to the Romans."

_____ a. When was the epistle to the Romans written?

_____ b. What could be some of the purposes of the epistle?

_____ c. What are the four main parts of the epistle?

_____ d. What great controversy existed in the Church at this time?

_____ e. When was this matter settled theologically?

_____ f. Why was it hard for some Church members to discontinue keeping the ordinances of the law of Moses?

_____ g. Where did Paul point as the source of eternal life?

Romans 1

VERSE NUMBER

_____ a. How was Jesus Christ declared to be the Son of God?

_____ b. To whom is the epistle addressed?

_____ c. What does Paul request in his prayers? Why?

_____ d. Why was Paul not ashamed of the gospel of Jesus Christ?

_____ e. Against whom is the wrath of God revealed? (See also Romans 1:18b.)

_____ f. Why are they without excuse?

_____ g. What did mankind do when they knew God? (See also v. 21b.)

_____ h. What did God deliver them up to do?

_____ i. How did Paul describe those who had rejected God?

Romans 2

_____ a. Why do we condemn ourselves when we judge others?

_____ b. Where does the goodness of God lead us?

_____ c. What will be rendered to everyone on the Day of Judgment?

_____ d. Who will be justified before God?

_____ e. How did the Jews see themselves?

_____ f. What should we be careful not to do?

_____ g. Who is a true Jew?

Romans 3

_____ a. By what is man not justified? (See headnote to Romans 3.)

_____ b. How is justification made possible? (See headnote.)

_____ c. What is the advantage of being a Jew from the heart? (See also v. 1a.)

_____ d. To whom does the punishment of the law apply?

Romans 4

_____ a. What was counted unto Abraham for righteousness? (See also Romans 4:2a; headnote.)

_____ b. What is required of us to be justified? (See v. 16a; see also headnote.)

_____ c. To whom is the promise of Abraham made? (See v. 16a.)

_____ d. In whom must we believe to have righteousness counted unto us?

Romans 5

_____ a. How can we have peace with God?

_____ b. What does tribulation lead to?

_____ c. What does patience teach?

_____ d. What does experience teach?

_____ e. What does hope do? Why?

_____ f. For whom did Christ die?

_____ g. What came upon all mankind by the sin of one?

_____ h. What came upon all mankind by the righteousness of one? (See also Bible Dictionary, p. 617, s.v. "Atonement.")

Romans 6

_____ a. List three things that baptism symbolizes. (See also headnote to Romans 6.)

_____ b. What is required of us so that sin will not have dominion over us? (See also v. 14a.)

_____ c. What reason did Paul give in verse 16 for not sinning? (See also Alma 34:33–36.)

_____ d. How did the Romans become servants of righteousness?

_____ e. What is the reward for sin?

_____ f. What is the reward for being free from sin?

Romans 7

VERSE NUMBER

_____ a. What was fulfilled in Christ? (See also headnote to Romans 7; Bible Dictionary, p. 722, s.v. "Law of Moses.")

_____ b. What worked to "bring forth fruit unto death"? (Romans 7:5; see v. 5a.)

_____ c. What does Paul delight in? (See also headnote.)

Romans 8

VERSE NUMBER

_____ a. What is the reward for being carnally minded? Why?

_____ b. What is the reward for being spiritually minded?

_____ c. Who are the sons of God? (See also D&C 25:1.)

_____ d. What do the sons of God become?

_____ e. For whom do all things work together for good?

_____ f. How strong was Paul's love of God?

Romans 9

VERSE NUMBER

_____ a. What does Paul teach the Romans in chapter 9? (See headnote to Romans 9.)

_____ b. What was Israel foreordained to receive? (See also headnote.)

_____ c. Why had Israel "not attained to the law of righteousness"? (V. 31.)

Romans 10

VERSE NUMBER

_____ a. To whom does salvation come? How? (See also headnote to Romans 10.)

_____ b. How does faith come? (See also headnote.)

_____ c. Why was Israel not saved?

Romans 11

_____ a. How was Israel chosen? (See headnote to Romans 11.)

_____ b. What are the gentiles grafted into? (See headnote.)

_____ c. When will the gospel go again to the Jews? (See headnote.)

_____ d. What does Paul think about God?

Romans 12

_____ a. How does Paul counsel the Saints "to present their bodies"? (Headnote to Romans 12.)

_____ b. How are we to think of ourselves?

_____ c. List six things we should be doing.

_____ d. How should we overcome evil?

Romans 13

_____ a. What does Paul counsel the Saints? (See headnote to Romans 13.)

_____ b. What should we be "unto the higher powers"? (V. 1; see also v. 1a.)

_____ c. What does verse 8 say about debt?

_____ d. What are we to cast off and then put on?

_____ e. How are we to walk? (See also v. 13a.)

Romans 14

_____ a. What are we to avoid doing? Why? (See also headnote to Romans 14.)

_____ b. What will every knee and tongue do? (See also v. 11b.)

_____ c. What does the kingdom of God embrace?

Romans 15

_____ a. How do true Saints act toward each other? (See also headnote to Romans 15; Bible Dictionary, p. 767, s.v. "Saint.")

_____ b. What was poured out upon the gentiles? (See also headnote to Romans 15.)

_____ c. What did Paul ask the members of the Church to pray for?

Romans 16

_____ a. Which members of the Church did Paul counsel the Romans to avoid? Why?

_____ b. What should we be wise about?

The First Epistle of Paul the Apostle to the Corinthians

Introduction

See Bible Dictionary, page 743, s.v. " Pauline Epistles—Epistle to the Corinthians."

_____ a. Why was Corinth a meeting point for many nationalities?

_____ b. From what nationality were most of Paul's converts in Corinth?

1 Corinthians 1

VERSE NUMBER

_____ a. To whom was the first epistle to the Corinthians written?

_____ b. What did Paul beseech his brethren in Corinth to do?

_____ c. How did the preaching of Christ affect the Jews? the Greeks? and the believers?

_____ d. What has God chosen the foolish and weak to do? (See also 1 Corinthians 1:27b.)

1 Corinthians 2

VERSE NUMBER

_____ a. What did Paul teach the Corinthians?

_____ b. Why did Paul speak "not with enticing words of man's wisdom"? (1 Corinthians 2:4.)

_____ c. What was revealed by the Spirit?

_____ d. Why is the Spirit essential to understanding the scriptures?

1 Corinthians 3

VERSE NUMBER

_____ a. Why did Paul speak to them as "babes in Christ"? (1 Corinthians 3:1.)

_____ b. How were the Corinthians carnal?

_____ c. What will test or prove every individual's work?

_____ d. Why are we to keep ourselves clean and pure?

_____ e. Why should we not trust "the wisdom of this world"? (V. 19.)

1 Corinthians 4

VERSE NUMBER

_____ a. What is required of the stewards of the gospel?

_____ b. Why should we not judge until the Second Coming?

_____ c. What did Paul say about the apostles?

_____ d. What choice did Paul give the Corinthians? (See also 1 Corinthians 4:21a.)

---

1 Corinthians 5

_____ a. What was reported to be among the Corinthians?

_____ b. What were they to do with the transgressor?

_____ c. How were the Corinthians to keep the Passover?

_____ d. Who were the Saints not to keep company with?

---

1 Corinthians 6

_____ a. What did Paul counsel the Saints to do about their grievances?

_____ b. Who will not inherit the kingdom of God?

_____ c. What does Paul counsel the Saints to flee from? Why?

---

1 Corinthians 7

_____ a. Who is Paul directing his message to? (See headnote to 1 Corinthians 7.)

_____ b. What are husband and wife to render to each other?

_____ c. Why are husband and wife not to separate? (See also v. 5a.)

_____ d. What is the command of the Lord in verses 10 and 11?

_____ e. Who is Paul speaking to in verse 29? (See v. 29a.)

_____ f. How is the married man hindered from serving the Lord? (See v. 29a.)

1 Corinthians 8

_____ a. What can knowledge do if we are not careful?

_____ b. What does charity do? (See 1 Corinthians 8:1c, d.)

_____ c. Who does Paul say is our God and who is our Lord?

_____ d. Why should we set a good example?

1 Corinthians 9

_____ a. Why did Paul rejoice? (See headnote to 1 Corinthians 9.)

_____ b. What has the Lord ordained concerning those that preach the gospel?

_____ c. How did Paul preach the gospel? (See also headnote.)

_____ d. Why did Paul become all things to all people? (See also headnote.)

_____ e. How does Paul keep his body in subjection? Why? (See v. 27a.)

1 Corinthians 10

_____ a. What is Christ to Israel? (See headnote to 1 Corinthians 10.)

_____ b. What did the Israelites do that the Corinthians were not to do?

_____ c. Why were these examples provided? (See v. 11b.)

_____ d. Why are we able to withstand temptation?

1 Corinthians 11

_____ a. What is Paul speaking of in 1 Corinthians 11:1–16? (See headnote.)

_____ b. Why are we to partake of the bread and the water? (See also 1 Corinthians 11:20a.)

_____ c. Why should we refrain from partaking of the sacrament unworthily?

_____ d. Why were many sick among the Corinthians?

---

1 Corinthians 12

_____ a. What key did Paul give the Corinthians?

_____ b. List ten gifts of the Spirit. (See also D&C 46:8–25; Moroni 10:8–17.)

_____ c. What has God set in his church?

_____ d. Why are we to seek earnestly for the best gifts? (See D&C 46:8.)

---

1 Corinthians 13

_____ a. What does Paul say about the importance of having charity?

_____ b. What does Paul say charity is? What does he say charity is not? (See Bible Dictionary, p. 632, s.v. "Charity.")

_____ c. What is greater than faith and hope?

---

1 Corinthians 14

_____ a. Why is it good to seek the gift of prophecy?

_____ b. Why should we seek spiritual gifts?

_____ c. What is God the author of?

---

1 Corinthians 15

_____ a. Who saw Christ after his resurrection, according to Paul?

_____ b. How was Christ the "firstfruits of them that slept"? (1 Corinthians 15:20.)

_____ c. Who is the last enemy to be destroyed?

_____ d. What vicarious ordinance were the Saints doing in the Church?

_____ e. List the three degrees of glory. (See v. 40a; Bible Dictionary, p. 655, s.v. "Degrees of Glory.")

_____ f. How do the degrees of glory differ? (See also D&C 76:50–113.)

_____ g. What is the sting of death?

_____ h. What did Paul admonish his brethren to do?

---

1 Corinthians 16

_____ a. How were the Corinthians to receive Timothy?

_____ b. What counsel did Paul give to the Corinthians? (See also 1 Corinthians 16:13d.)

The Second Epistle of Paul the Apostle to the Corinthians

Introduction

See Bible Dictionary, page 744, s.v. "Pauline Epistles – Epistle to the Corinthians."

_____ a. How was the first epistle to the Corinthians received?

_____ b. What had the Church done about the sexual offense?

_____ c. What had sprung up between Paul and his converts?

_____ d. List the five main parts of the second epistle to the Corinthians.

---

2 Corinthians 1

_____ a. What does God do for his Saints? (See headnote to 2 Corinthians 1.)

_____ b. What has happened to the Saints? (See headnote.)

2 Corinthians 2

_____ a. What should the Saints do for each other? Why? (See headnote to 2 Corinthians 2.)

_____ b. How will members of the Church always triumph?

2 Corinthians 3

_____ a. What surpasses the law of Moses? (See headnote to 2 Corinthians 3.)

_____ b. What is also present with the Spirit of the Lord? (See headnote.)

2 Corinthians 4

_____ a. What shines on the Saints? (See headnote to 2 Corinthians 4.)

_____ b. What is nothing in comparison to eternal glory? (See headnote.)

_____ c. What are things that are seen?

_____ d. What are things that are not seen?

2 Corinthians 5

_____ a. What do Saints walk by? (See headnote to 2 Corinthians 5.)

_____ b. What do Saints seek? (See headnote.)

_____ c. Who must appear before the judgment seat of Christ? Why?

_____ d. What does the gospel do? (See headnote; see also v. 16a.)

_____ e. What do God's ministers do? (See headnote.)

2 Corinthians 6

_____ a. What is this the day of?

_____ b. How must God's ministers act? (See headnote to 2 Corinthians 6.)

_____ c. What should the Saints refrain from doing?

2 Corinthians 7

_____ a. What does Paul encourage the Saints to do?

_____ b. What report did Titus bring to Paul about the Corinthians?

_____ c. What leads to repentance?

_____ d. What kind of sorrow leads to death?

_____ e. Why had Paul written previously to the Corinthians?

2 Corinthians 8

_____ a. What do true Saints do? (See headnote to 2 Corinthians 8.)

_____ b. What did Christ bring out of his poverty? (See headnote.)

2 Corinthians 9

_____ a. What will happen to one who sows bountifully?

_____ b. How should we give? Why?

2 Corinthians 10

_____ a. What should we bring into obedience? (See also headnote to 2 Corinthians 10.)

_____ b. Who is commended for his work?

---

2 Corinthians 11

VERSE NUMBER

_____ a. Why did Paul fear for the Corinthians?

_____ b. Who did Satan send to deceive them? (See also headnote to 2 Corinthians 11.)

_____ c. What can Satan be transformed into? (See also D&C 128:20; Bible Dictionary, p. 656, s.v. "Devil.")

_____ d. How are we able to detect Satan if he appears to us? (See D&C 129:4–8.)

_____ e. List four things that Paul had suffered, as recorded in 2 Corinthians 11:24–25.

---

2 Corinthians 12

VERSE NUMBER

_____ a. Where was Paul taken? (See also headnote to 2 Corinthians 12; v. 2a, c.)

_____ b. Why does the Lord give people weakness? (See also headnote; Ether 12:27.)

_____ c. What had Paul done among the Corinthians? (See also headnote to 2 Corinthians 12.)

_____ d. Why did Paul fear for the Corinthians?

---

2 Corinthians 13

VERSE NUMBER

_____ a. How shall every word be established?

_____ b. In 2 Corinthians 13:5, what did Paul tell the Corinthians to do? (See also headnote.)

_____ c. In verse 11, what did Paul counsel the Saints to do? Why?

The Epistle of Paul the Apostle to the Galatians

Introduction

See Bible Dictionary, page 744, s.v. "Pauline Epistles—Epistle to the Galatians."

_____ a. When were the Galatian churches visited by Paul?

_____ b. Why did Paul probably write the epistle to the Galatians?

_____ c. What does Paul do in this epistle?

_____ d. What are the five main sections of this epistle?

Galatians 1

_____ a. Why did Paul marvel?

_____ b. What did Paul certify to the Galatians? (See also Galatians 1:11a.)

_____ c. How long after Paul's conversion did he go to Jerusalem?

_____ d. Which apostles did Paul see during his first visit to Jerusalem after his conversion?

Galatians 2

_____ a. How long was it before Paul went the second time to Jerusalem?

_____ b. What did Paul report in Jerusalem? (See also Galatians 2:2b.)

_____ c. Who did the brethren in Jerusalem want Paul to remember?

Galatians 3

_____ a. What did God give to Abraham? (See also headnote to Galatians 3.)

_____ b. Why was the law of Moses given?

_____ c. Who are Abraham's seed? (See also headnote.)

Galatians 4

_____ a. How have the Saints become the children of God? (See headnote to Galatians 4; D&C 25:1.)

_____ b. To whom does Paul call the Galatians back? (See headnote to Galatians 4.)

Galatians 5

_____ a. What were the Galatians to stand fast in?

_____ b. What works by love?

_____ c. How are we to use our liberty? Why?

_____ d. What are the works of the flesh?

_____ e. Those who live after the manner of the flesh will not inherit what?

_____ f. What are the fruits of the Spirit?

_____ g. What challenge does Paul give the members of the Church?

Galatians 6

_____ a. What must the strong do for the weak?

_____ b. Whose burdens should we bear?

_____ c. How will we be rewarded?

_____ d. What should we "be not weary" of? (Galatians 6:9.)

The Epistle of Paul the Apostle to the Ephesians

Introduction

See Bible Dictionary, page 746, s.v. "Pauline Epistles—Epistle to the Ephesians."

_____ a. Why is the epistle to the Ephesians of great importance?

_____ b. List the four main sections of this epistle.

Ephesians 1

_____ a. What were the Saints foreordained to receive? (See headnote to Ephesians 1.)

_____ b. What will be restored in the latter days? (See headnote.)

_____ c. By what are the Saints sealed? (See also headnote.)

_____ d. How are the Ephesians to know God and Christ? (See also headnote.)

Ephesians 2

_____ a. How are we saved? (See also Bible Dictionary, p. 669, s.v. "Faith"; p. 697, s.v. "Grace.")

_____ b. What saves Jew and Gentile alike? (See headnote.)

_____ c. Upon what foundation is the Church built?

Ephesians 3

_____ a. Who are made fellow heirs with Israel by the gospel?

_____ b. What did Paul desire for the Ephesians?

Ephesians 4

_____ a. How are we to act? Why?

_____ b. What is the purpose of the apostles, prophets, evangelists, pastors, and teachers? (See also Bible Dictionary, p. 645, s.v. "Church"; p. 668, s.v. "Evangelist.")

_____ c. What are the Saints not to do?

_____ d. List ten things that Paul exhorted the Saints to do.

_____ e. What are the Saints sealed to?

Ephesians 5

_____ a. Who have no inheritance in the kingdom of God?

_____ b. What will the children of disobedience experience?

_____ c. What type of relationship should exist between husband and wife?

Ephesians 6

_____ a. What should children do?

_____ b. What should fathers do?

_____ c. Who are judged by the same law? (See headnote to Ephesians 6.)

_____ d. What should the Saints put on? Why?

_____ e. Who do we wrestle against?

_____ f. What are the two weapons a member of the Church must use to win the battle against Satan?

The Epistle of Paul the Apostle to the Philippians

Introduction

See Bible Dictionary, page 745, s.v. "Pauline Epistles—Epistle to the Philippians."

_____ a. How many years long was the interval between the second and the third group of epistles? Why?

_____ b. Where was Paul when the third group of epistles was written?

_____ c. What did Paul's converts do after his first visit?

_____ d. What did they do when they heard Paul was a prisoner in Rome?

_____ e. What is the main purpose of the epistle to the Philippians?

_____ f. List the six main sections of the epistle.

Philippians 1

_____ a. What did Paul pray for?

_____ b. How did Paul's imprisonment affect the gospel cause?

_____ c. What was Paul hard pressed to choose between? (See also Philippians 1:23a.)

_____ d. How should we conduct ourselves?

Philippians 2

_____ a. How should the Saints act?

_____ b. What did Paul say that every knee must do and every tongue confess?

_____ c. What must the Saints do? (See also headnote to Philippians 2.)

_____ d. How are we to conduct ourselves? Why?

_____ e. How does Paul face martyrdom? (See also headnote.)

Philippians 3

_____ a. What does Paul tell the Saints to beware of?

_____ b. What did Paul do for Christ? (See headnote to Philippians 3.)

_____ c. What do true ministers do? (See also headnote.)

Philippians 4

_____ a. What did Paul counsel the Saints to do?

_____ b. How are we to make our requests known to God?

_____ c. What will be the result?

_____ d. What things should we seek after?

The Epistle of Paul the Apostle to the Colossians

Introduction

See Bible Dictionary, page 746, s.v. "Pauline Epistles—Epistle to the Colossians."

_____ a. What did Epaphras report?

_____ b. Why was that teaching attractive?

_____ c. What is the only way that sanctification may be obtained?

_____ d. What are the four main sections of the epistle to the Colossians?

Colossians 1

_____ a. To whom is the epistle written?

_____ b. List five things that Paul and Timothy prayed for, as recorded in Colossians 1:9–11.

_____ c. Who created all things that are in heaven and in earth? (See also v. 16*d*.)

_____ d. Who was the first to be resurrected? Why?

Colossians 2

_____ a. In what way was Paul with the Colossians?

_____ b. What should we beware of?

Colossians 3

_____ a. For what are we to seek? How?

_____ b. In Colossians 3:12–17, what are the Saints exhorted to do?

_____ c. What should wives do?

_____ d. What should husbands do?

_____ e. What should children do?

_____ f. What should fathers do?

_____ g. How should we use our talents?

Colossians 4

_____ a. List five things Paul exhorted the Saints to do.

_____ b. What did Paul call Luke?

The First Epistle of Paul the Apostle to the Thessalonians

Introduction

See Bible Dictionary, page 743, s.v. "Pauline Epistles—Epistle to the Thessalonians."

_____ a. Where and when was the first epistle to the Thessalonians written?

_____ b. Where is the account of Paul's visit to Thessalonica?

_____ c. What did Paul do when he was unable to return?

_____ d. What is this first epistle the outcome of?

_____ e. What are the two main sections of the epistle?

---

1 Thessalonians 1

VERSE NUMBER

_____ a. How was the gospel delivered to the Thessalonians?

_____ b. How did the Saints in Thessalonica receive the gospel?

---

1 Thessalonians 2

VERSE NUMBER

_____ a. How did Paul and his companions preach the gospel to them?

_____ b. What is the relationship of converts to the missionaries?

---

1 Thessalonians 3

VERSE NUMBER

_____ a. Why was Timotheus sent to them?

_____ b. What did Timotheus report about the Thessalonians?

_____ c. What was Paul's prayer for the Saints?

---

1 Thessalonians 4

VERSE NUMBER

_____ a. What did Paul exhort the Saints to do? (See headnote to 1 Thessalonians 4.)

_____ b. What will happen at the Second Coming? (See also vv. 15a, 17a.)

1 Thessalonians 5

_____ a. Why were the Saints to watch for the Second Coming?

_____ b. List seven things the Saints were exhorted in 1 Thessalonians 5:11–17 to do.

_____ c. What are we not to despise?

_____ d. What should we hold fast to?

_____ e. What should we abstain from?

The Second Epistle of Paul the Apostle to the Thessalonians

Introduction

See Bible Dictionary, page 743, s.v. "Pauline Epistles—Epistle to the Thessalonians."

_____ a. What happened during the time between 1 and 2 Thessalonians?

_____ b. What fostered the unhealthy excitement?

_____ c. What had been misunderstood?

_____ d. What are the six main sections of the second epistle to the Thessalonians?

2 Thessalonians 1

_____ a. Why does Paul thank God for the Thessalonians?

b. What will the Lord do at the Second Coming?

---

2 Thessalonians 2

_____ a. What does the gospel prepare people for? (See headnote to 2 Thessalonians 2.)

_____ b. What will precede the Second Coming? (See also v. 7a.)

_____ c. What were the brethren to do?

---

2 Thessalonians 3

_____ a. What were the Thessalonians to pray for?

_____ b. What had Paul commanded about those who refused to work?

_____ c. What should we "be not weary" of? (2 Thessalonians 3:13.)

The First Epistle of Paul the Apostle to Timothy

Introduction

See Bible Dictionary, page 747, s.v. "Pauline Epistles — 1 Timothy."

_____ a. Why was the first epistle to Timothy written?

_____ b. What are the eight main sections of the epistle?

---

1 Timothy 1

_____ a. What was Timothy exhorted to do? (See headnote to 1 Timothy 1.)

_____ b. What had some of the Saints done? (See also v. 6a.)

_____ c. Why did Paul receive mercy from God for persecuting the Saints?

_____ d. Who did Christ come to save?

_____ e. What charge did Paul give to Timothy?

---

1 Timothy 2

VERSE NUMBER

_____ a. For whom should we pray? Why?

_____ b. Who is our mediator?

_____ c. How were the women to dress? (See also headnote to 1 Timothy 2.)

_____ d. What did Paul admonish the sisters to do? (See also v. 15a.)

---

1 Timothy 3

VERSE NUMBER

_____ a. What priesthood offices in the Church does Paul list the qualifications for? (See headnote to 1 Timothy 3.)

_____ b. What were the qualifications for a bishop?

_____ c. What were the qualifications for a deacon?

---

1 Timothy 4

VERSE NUMBER

_____ a. What did Paul describe in 1 Timothy 4? (See headnote.)

_____ b. What will some do who depart from the faith in the last days?

_____ c. Compared with godliness, what does "bodily exercise" profit us? (V. 8; see also v. 8a.)

_____ d. Why is godliness profitable?

_____ e. What was Timothy to be doing? Why?

1 Timothy 5

_____ a. Who were the Saints to care for? (See headnote to 1 Timothy 5.)

_____ b. Who are they who have "denied the faith, and [are] worse than an infidel"? (V. 8.)

_____ c. What were the younger women to do?

_____ d. Which elders were "counted worthy of double honour"? (V. 17.)

1 Timothy 6

_____ a. What is the risk of desiring to be rich? (See also 1 Timothy 6:9a.)

_____ b. What is the root of all evil?

_____ c. What should we follow after?

_____ d. What charge did Paul give to the rich?

The Second Epistle of Paul the Apostle to Timothy

Introduction

See Bible Dictionary, page 748, s.v. "Pauline Epistles—2 Timothy."

_____ a. When was 2 Timothy written?

_____ b. What does this epistle contain?

_____ c. List the seven main sections of the epistle.

2 Timothy 1

_____ a. What has Christ brought through the gospel?

_____ b. What did Paul say of the Saints in Asia?

---

2 Timothy 2

_____ a. What was Timothy to commit to faithful men? Why?

_____ b. For whom does Paul endure all things? Why?

_____ c. Why should we study the scriptures?

_____ d. What are we to shun? Why? (See also 2 Timothy 2:16a, 17a.)

_____ e. What are we to seek?

_____ f. What are the servants of the Lord to do?

---

2 Timothy 3

_____ a. How did Paul describe men in our day?

_____ b. What did Paul say the members would do in the churches in Asia?

_____ c. What did Paul counsel Timothy to do in the perilous days ahead?

_____ d. How is scripture given? Why? (See 2 Timothy 3:16a.)

_____ e. What is scripture to be used for?

---

2 Timothy 4

_____ a. What solemn charge did Paul give to Timothy? Why? (See also headnote to 2 Timothy 4; v. 2b.)

_____ b. What did Paul say of his missionary effort?

_____ c. Who are assured of exaltation? (See also headnote.)

_____ d. What has the Lord done to preserve Paul? Why?

_____ e. Who was "ordained the first bishop of the church of the Ephesians"? (Endnote.)

The Epistle of Paul to Titus

Introduction

See Bible Dictionary, p. 747, s.v. "Pauline Epistles—Epistle to Titus."

_____ a. What are the six main sections of the epistle to Titus?

See Bible Dictionary, p. 785, s.v. "Titus."

_____ a. Who converted Titus? Where?

_____ b. Where had Paul sent Titus?

_____ c. Where was Titus when he received Paul's epistle?

_____ d. Where was Titus later sent on a mission? (See also Map 22.)

Titus 1

VERSE NUMBER

_____ a. When was eternal life promised?

_____ b. What are the qualifications of a bishop?

_____ c. What do the "vain talkers and deceivers" do? (Titus 1:10.) Why?

_____ d. What are all things to the pure? (See also v. 15a.)

_____ e. How do the defiled deny God?

Titus 2

VERSE NUMBER

_____ a. What should the Saints do? (See headnote to Titus 2.)

_____ b. How were the aged men to act?

_____ c. How were the aged women to act? Why?

_____ d. How were the young men to act?

_____ e. What has the grace of God taught people to do?

Titus 3

_____ a. What must the Saints do after baptism? (See headnote to Titus 3.)

_____ b. How were the Saints to act?

_____ c. How were the Saints brought to the knowledge of God and saved?

_____ d. What were the Saints to avoid?

_____ e. Who was "ordained the first bishop of the church of the Cretians"? (Endnote.)

The Epistle of Paul to Philemon

Introduction

See Bible Dictionary, page 746, s.v. "Pauline Epistles—Epistle to Philemon."

_____ a. What is the epistle to Philemon?

_____ b. What did Paul do about the matter?

_____ c. What did Paul ask in this epistle?

Philemon 1

_____ a. What does the gospel change a servant into? (See headnote to Philemon 1.)

_____ b. What does Paul request for Onesimus?

The Epistle of Paul the Apostle to the Hebrews

Introduction

See Bible Dictionary, page 746, s.v. "Pauline Epistle—Epistle to the Hebrews."

_____ a. To whom was the epistle written? Why?

_____ b. What did Paul find when he returned to Jerusalem from his third mission?

_____ c. What had the conference at Jerusalem concluded ten years earlier?

_____ d. What are the ten main sections of the epistle to the Hebrews?

_____ e. What is the characteristic doctrine of the third group of epistles?

_____ f. What is the gospel shown to do?

Hebrews 1

VERSE NUMBER

_____ a. What has God done "in many locations and various ways"? (Hebrews 1:1a.)

_____ b. What had God done in Paul's day?

_____ c. Who made the worlds?

_____ d. How is Christ above the angels? (See also headnote to Hebrews 1.)

_____ e. What did Jesus do in the beginning?

_____ f. What are angels to do? (See also v. 6b.)

Hebrews 2

VERSE NUMBER

_____ a. List three things Jesus came to do. (See headnote to Hebrews 2.)

_____ b. How did the Saints know of the plan of salvation?

_____ c. Why did Jesus come into the world and take upon him flesh and blood?

Hebrews 3

_____ a. How does Paul refer to Christ? (See also headnote to Hebrews 3.)

_____ b. Why was God grieved with the children of Israel who came out of Egypt?

_____ c. What should we beware of?

_____ d. Why should we exhort one another daily? (See also Alma 34:39.)

_____ e. Why could the children of Israel not enter into the promised land?

Hebrews 4

_____ a. Why did ancient Israel reject the gospel?

_____ b. What has God sworn to do? (See Hebrews 4:3a.)

_____ c. How did Paul describe the word of God?

_____ d. Why is Jesus able to understand our imperfections?

Hebrews 5

_____ a. What is the role of a high priest?

_____ b. How does a man become a high priest?

_____ c. Who called Christ to be a high priest?

_____ d. How did Jesus learn obedience?

_____ e. Who is strong doctrine for?

Hebrews 6

_____ a. For whom is it impossible to be renewed again unto repentance? Why? (See headnote to Hebrews 6; v. 3*a*.)

_____ b. How will the earth be cleansed? (See v. 3*a*.)

_____ c. What is the fate of those who do not bring forth good fruit? (See v. 3*a*.)

_____ d. What will God not forget? (See v. 3*a*.)

_____ e. When did Abraham receive the promise of eternal life? (See also v. 14*a*.)

Hebrews 7

_____ a. What does the Melchizedek Priesthood do? (See headnote to Hebrews 7; see also Bible Dictionary, p. 730, s.v. "Melchizedek Priesthood.")

_____ b. How is the Melchizedek Priesthood received? (See headnote; v. 19*a*.)

_____ c. How does salvation come? (See headnote.)

_____ d. List five things we learn about Melchizedek in verses 1 and 2. (See also JST Genesis 14.)

_____ e. Even though the Levitical, or Aaronic, priesthood administered the law of Moses, holders of that priesthood could not bring an individual to what? What else was necessary?

_____ f. How was Jesus different from the Jewish high priests? (See Hebrews 7:26*a*.)

Hebrews 8

_____ a. What did Christ offer himself as a sacrifice for? (See headnote to Hebrews 8; v. 4*a*.)

_____ b. What was the new covenant God promised to make with Israel?

Hebrews 9

_____ a. What did the ordinances of the law of Moses symbolize? (See headnote to Hebrews 9.)

_____ b. What is Christ the mediator of? (See also v. 15c.)

_____ c. Where has Christ entered? Why?

Hebrews 10

_____ a. How are we sanctified? (See also headnote to Hebrews 10.)

_____ b. In verse 22, what did Paul encourage the Hebrews to do? (See also v. 22d.)

_____ c. Who are damned? (See also headnote.)

_____ d. What do the just live by?

Hebrews 11

_____ a. How are we to understand the word and the work of God? (See headnote to Hebrews 11.)

_____ b. Whose faith was centered on Christ? (See headnote.)

_____ c. What have men done by faith? (See headnote.)

_____ d. What is faith? (See also v. 1b.)

_____ e. List fifteen things listed in verses 3 through 11 and 17 through 31 that Paul said were accomplished through faith.

_____ f. Why is faith necessary to please God?

_____ g. What trials had some people passed through because of their faith in Christ, as recorded in verses 35 through 38?

_____ h. Why are people required to suffer? (See v. 40a.)

Hebrews 12

_____ a. In Hebrews 12:1–2, what did Paul encourage the Hebrews to do?

_____ b. Who does the Lord chasten? Why?

_____ c. Who is the father of our spirits?

_____ d. What is one of the requirements to see God?

_____ e. Who belongs to the church of the firstborn? (See also headnote.)

Hebrews 13

_____ a. How are we to live?

_____ b. How does Paul view marriage?

_____ c. What should we boldly say?

_____ d. Why did Jesus die on the cross outside Jerusalem?

_____ e. How are we to offer an acceptable sacrifice to God?

_____ f. Why should we sustain Church leaders?

The General Epistle of James

Introduction

See Bible Dictionary, page 709, s.v. "James, Epistle of."

_____ a. Who is the writer generally thought to be?

VERSE NUMBER

_____ b. Who is the epistle of James directed to?

_____ c. List six important teachings found in this epistle.

James 1

VERSE NUMBER

_____ a. To whom is James writing?

_____ b. What are we to do if we lack wisdom? (See also Joseph Smith–History 1:11.)

_____ c. How are we to ask?

_____ d. Why are we blessed when we resist temptation? (See also James 1:12b.)

_____ e. When are we tempted?

_____ f. How do we become spiritually dead?

_____ g. What must we do to prevent ourselves from being deceived?

_____ h. When does our religion become vain?

_____ i. What is pure and undefiled religion?

James 2

VERSE NUMBER

_____ a. Why should we respect the poor? (See James 2:1a, 4a.)

_____ b. What is the royal law that we should obey?

_____ c. What must we do for our faith to be alive?

_____ d. How are we justified?

James 3

VERSE NUMBER

_____ a. What can "a very small helm" do for a ship? (James 3:4.)

_____ b. What can a little fire do to a forest? (See also v. 5b.)

_____ c. Why should we be careful about what we say?

_____ d. What accompanies envy and strife?

_____ e. How can we recognize wisdom from above?

James 4

_____ a. Why are there wars and fighting?

_____ b. Why do we fail to receive things we pray for?

_____ c. What is required for the devil to flee from us?

_____ d. Why should we refrain from speaking evil of one another?

_____ e. What should be our attitude instead of boasting? Why?

_____ f. What is sin?

James 5

_____ a. What miseries will come upon the wanton rich? Why?

_____ b. What are the prophets of the Lord a good example of?

_____ c. What are we to do when we are sick?

_____ d. List two things the prayer of faith will do for the sick.

_____ e. Why should we be righteous and pray fervently?

_____ f. What are two good reasons to be active in missionary work?

The Epistles of Peter

Introduction

See Bible Dictionary, page 749, s.v. "Peter, Epistles of."

_____ a. From where and when was the first epistle of Peter written?

_____ b. To whom was it addressed?

_____ c. What was the purpose of this epistle?

_____ d. What other valuable teachings are contained in this epistle? (See Bible Dictionary, p. 760, s.v. "Regeneration.")

_____ e. List four topics you consider important in this epistle.

See Bible Dictionary, page 750, s.v. "Peter, Epistles of."

_____ a. To whom was the second epistle of Peter written?

_____ b. What problem did this epistle aim to guard against?

_____ c. What did Peter explain in chapter 1?

_____ d. What did Peter discuss in chapter 2?

_____ e. What did Peter reaffirm in chapter 3?

_____ f. What did Joseph Smith say about Peter's writings?

The First Epistle General of Peter

1 Peter 1

VERSE NUMBER

_____ a. What is reserved in heaven for the faithful Saints?

_____ b. What is "much more precious than of gold"? (1 Peter 1:7.)

_____ c. How will the Father judge us?

_____ d. How are we to be redeemed?

_____ e. How had the Saints purified their souls?

1 Peter 2

VERSE NUMBER

_____ a. What are we to lay aside when seeking the word of God?

_____ b. How did Peter describe his readers?

_____ c. What are we to abstain from?

_____ d. Why should our "conversation [be] honest among the Gentiles"? (1 Peter 2:12.)

_____ e. Why were the Saints to obey their governments?

_____ f. How should we suffer wrongs? Why? (See also v. 19b.)

1 Peter 3

_____ a. What did Peter instruct wives to do? Why?

_____ b. What did Peter instruct husbands to do? Why?

_____ c. How were the Saints to deal with each other? Why?

_____ d. How should we bear suffering for righteousness' sake?

_____ e. What did Jesus do for the spirits in prison? (See also D&C 138.)

1 Peter 4

_____ a. How should we live the rest of our time in the flesh? (See 1 Peter 4:1b.)

_____ b. Why is the gospel preached to those who live in the spirit world? (See v. 6a.)

_____ c. Why should we have charity? (See v. 8a.)

_____ d. Where was the judgment to begin? (See also D&C 112:24–28.)

1 Peter 5

_____ a. What did Peter instruct the elders to do?

_____ b. How where the elders to do that?

_____ c. How were the younger Saints to act?

The Second Epistle General of Peter

---

2 Peter 1

VERSE NUMBER

_____ a. What is required for us to know Jesus?

_____ b. What is our condition if we do not have these things?

_____ c. In 2 Peter 1:10, what does Paul exhort the Saints to do? (See also D&C 131:5.)

_____ d. What had Jesus shown to Peter?

_____ e. How did God the Father introduce his Son on the mount?

_____ f. How is true prophecy received?

---

2 Peter 2

VERSE NUMBER

_____ a. What will false teachers do among the Saints?

_____ b. What does the Lord know how to do?

_____ c. Who will perish in their own corruption? (See headnote to 2 Peter 2.)

_____ d. How will those speak who corrupt?

_____ e. Why is the proverb in verse 22 true?

---

2 Peter 3

VERSE NUMBER

_____ a. What type of people will come in the last days? (See 2 Peter 3:3a.)

_____ b. What is the measure of a day to the Lord?

_____ c. Why is the Lord long suffering toward us?

_____ d. What will happen during the Lord's second coming? (See also v. 3a.)

_____ e. What counsel did Peter give us in verses 17 and 18?

The Epistles of John

Introduction

See Bible Dictionary, page 715, s.v. "John, Epistles of."

_____ a. What does the first epistle of John emphasize?

_____ b. What warnings does it contain?

_____ c. What does the second epistle condemn?

_____ d. What three men are referred to in the third epistle?

The First Epistle General of John

---

1 John 1

VERSE NUMBER

_____ a. What does John declare to the reader? Why?

_____ b. How do the Saints gain fellowship with God? (See also headnote to 1 John 1.)

_____ c. What is wrong with saying "we have no sin"? (1 John 1:8.)

_____ d. What must we do to gain forgiveness? (See also headnote.)

---

1 John 2

VERSE NUMBER

_____ a. Why is John writing these things?

_____ b. Who is our advocate with the Father? (See headnote to 1 John 2; v. 1a, b.)

_____ c. How can we know God? (See headnote.)

_____ d. Who "abideth in the light"? (V. 10.)

_____ e. Why are we not to love the world?

_____ f. What is an antichrist? (See also Bible Dictionary, p. 609, s.v. "Antichrist.")

---

1 John 3

_____ a. Who shall become like Christ? (See also headnote to 1 John 3.)

_____ b. What is sin?

_____ c. Why did Cain slay Abel?

_____ d. What dwells in those who help the needy?

_____ e. How can we have confidence toward God?

_____ f. What is required of us to get answers to our prayers?

---

1 John 4

_____ a. What was one way John said the members of the Church should try the spirits who come to them? (See also D&C 129.)

_____ b. How are we able to overcome the world?

_____ c. Why are we to love one another?

_____ d. Who has seen God? (See 1 John 4:12a.)

_____ e. What casts out fear?

_____ f. What is required of those who love God?

---

1 John 5

_____ a. How are the Saints born of God? (See headnote to 1 John 5.)

_____ b. What is required to gain eternal life? (See headnote.)

_____ c. What is required to love God? (See also John 14:15.)

_____ d. Why has John written these things?

_____ e. What confidence did John have in the Lord?

The Second Epistle of John

2 John 1

_____ a. Why did John rejoice greatly? (See also headnote to 2 John 1.)

_____ b. How did John define love?

The Third Epistle of John

3 John 1

_____ a. Why did John commend Gaius? (See also headnote to 3 John 1.)

_____ b. What was Gaius to follow after?

The General Epistle of Jude

Introduction

See Bible Dictionary, p. 719, s.v. "Jude, Epistle of."

_____ a. Who is Jude?

_____ b. To whom is the epistle of Jude addressed?

_____ c. What did Jude desire to do in his epistle?

Jude 1

_____ a. For what were Jude's "beloved" to earnestly contend for?

_____ b. Describe those who had crept into the church.

_____ c. What did some angels fail to keep?

_____ d. What did Michael dispute with Satan about? (See also Jude 1:9a.)

_____ e. What did Enoch prophesy? (See also headnote.)

The Revelation of St John the Divine

Introduction

See Bible Dictionary, page 762, s.v. "Revelation of John."

_____ a. What is the message of the book of Revelation?

_____ b. What did Joseph Smith say of the book of Revelation?

_____ c. List three guidelines to understanding the book of Revelation.

_____ d. List ten points of doctrine that are addressed in the book of Revelation.

_____ e. Where was John when he received this revelation?

Revelation 1

_____ a. Who are they who are blessed? (See Revelation 1:1a.)

_____ b. Who was the testimony of John directed to? (See v. 1*a*.)

_____ c. What has Christ chosen his Saints to be? (See headnote; v. 1*a*.)

_____ d. How will the Lord appear at his second coming? (See v. 1*a*.)

_____ e. How did John describe Jesus?

Revelation 2

VERSE NUMBER

_____ a. What is to happen to those who overcome the world? (See headnote to Revelation 2.)

_____ b. What was the servant in Ephesus commended for doing?

_____ c. What did the Lord tell the servant in Ephesus to do? Why? (See also vv. 1*b*, 4*a*.)

_____ d. What did the Lord tell the servant in Smyrna to do? Why? (See also v. 10*e*.)

_____ e. What did the Lord tell the servant in Pergamos to do? Why?

_____ f. What will the white stone mentioned in verse 17 help the Saints do? (See v. 17*c*.)

_____ g. What did the Lord tell the servant in Thyatira to do?

_____ h. What is to happen to those who overcome the world and keep the commandments? (See v. 26*a*.)

Revelation 3

VERSE NUMBER

_____ a. What promise is given to those who overcome the world? (See headnote to Revelation 3.)

_____ b. What did the Lord tell the servant in Sardis to do?

_____ c. What did the Lord tell the servant in Philadelphia he would do? Why?

_____ d. What did the Lord tell the Laodiceans?

_____ e. What promise did the Lord give if we will hear his voice and open the door?

Revelation 4

VERSE NUMBER

_____ a. What does John see? (See headnote to Revelation 4.)

_____ b. Who were the twenty-four elders "round about the throne"? (V. 4; see v. 4c.)

_____ c. What is the sea of glass spoken of in verse 6? (See v. 6a.)

_____ d. What are the four beasts mentioned in verse 6? (See v. 6c.)

_____ e. What is represented by the eyes and wings of the beast? (See D&C 77:4.)

Revelation 5

VERSE NUMBER

_____ a. What did John see in Revelation 5? (See also headnote.)

_____ b. What is contained in the book that John saw? (See v. 1b.)

_____ c. Who was found worthy to open the book? (See also v. 9b.)

_____ d. What did John hear every creature doing? (See also headnote.)

Revelation 6

VERSE NUMBER

_____ a. What did Jesus do? (See headnote to Revelation 6.)

_____ b. What are we to understand by the seven seals that sealed the book? (See v. 3a.)

_____ c. What did John see in the first seal?

_____ d. What did John see in the second seal?

_____ e. What did John see in the third seal?

_____ f. What did John see in the fourth seal?

_____ g. What did John see in the fifth seal? (See headnote.)

_____ h. What did John see in the sixth seal? (See headnote.)

Revelation 7

VERSE NUMBER

_____ a. List three things John saw in the sixth seal. (See headnote to Revelation 7.)

Who are the four angels mentioned in verse 1? (See v. 1*a*.)

_____ c. Who is the angel spoken of in verse 2? (See v. 2*a*.)

_____ d. What will this angel do? (See v. 2*a*.)

_____ e. When will these things be accomplished? (See D&C 77:10.)

_____ f. What are we to understand by the sealing of the one hundred forty-four thousand? (See Revelation 7:4*a*.)

_____ g. Who were arrayed in white robes?

_____ h. What did John learn further about them?

Revelation 8

VERSE NUMBER

_____ a. What does John see during the seventh seal? (See headnote to Revelation 8.)

_____ b. What are we to understand by the sounding of the seven trumpets? (See v. 2*a*.)

Revelation 9

VERSE NUMBER

_____ a. What did John see and record in Revelation 9? (See headnote.)

_____ b. Who were the locusts to torment?

_____ c. What happened when the sixth angel sounded his trumpet?

_____ d. When are these things to be accomplished? (See D&C 77:13.)

Revelation 10

VERSE NUMBER

_____ a. What was John commissioned to do? (See headnote to Revelation 10.)

_____ b. What was John told not to write?

_____ c. What did the angel declare that there should be no longer?

_____ d. What was the meaning of the little book that was eaten by John? (See Revelation 10:10a.)

_____ e. What did the angel say to John in verse 11? (See also D&C 7.)

Revelation 11

_____ a. What will happen to the two prophets in Jerusalem? (See headnote to Revelation 11.)

_____ b. How long will the gentiles tread Jerusalem?

_____ c. Who are the two witnesses spoken of in verse 3? (See v. 3b.)

_____ d. How long will the Lord's two prophets prophesy in Jerusalem?

_____ e. What power will they have?

_____ f. What will happen to the two prophets when they have finished their testimony?

_____ g. What will happen to them after they lie in the street for three and a half days?

_____ h. What will happen after they ascend to heaven?

_____ i. What did the voices in heaven say when the seventh angel sounded his trumpet?

_____ j. What did the twenty-four elders say?

Revelation 12

_____ a. List three things John sees in Revelation 12. (See headnote.)

_____ b. Who is the woman described in verses 1 through 6? (See v. 1a.)

_____ c. Who is the man child the woman delivered? (See v. 1a; see also Bible Dictionary, p. 763, no. 6, s.v. "Revelation of John.")

_____ d. Who was the great red dragon? (See Revelation 12:1a.)

_____ e. How did the brethren overcome Satan in the premortal earth life? (See v. 1a.)

_____ f. Where did the devil go when he was cast out? (See v. 1a.)

_____ g. Who does the devil seek to make war with on the earth? (See v. 1a.)

Revelation 13

_____ a. What do the "fierce looking beasts" represent? (See headnote; Revelation 13:1a.)

_____ b. What power was given to the beast?

_____ c. Who will worship the beast?

_____ d. How does the devil deceive men?

_____ e. What will happen to those who will not worship the image of the beast?

_____ f. Who will be able to buy and sell in that day?

_____ g. What is the number of the beast?

Revelation 14

_____ a. Where will Jesus stand? (See headnote to Revelation 14.)

_____ b. How was the gospel to be restored in the last days? (See headnote.)

_____ c. What did the first angel say? (See also Bible Dictionary, p. 763, no. 7, s.v. "Revelation of John.")

_____ d. What did the second angel say?

_____ e. What did the third angel say?

_____ f. What was John told to write?

Revelation 15

_____ a. What will the exalted Saints do? (See headnote to Revelation 15.)

_____ b. What did the seven angels have?

_____ c. Who did John see standing on the sea of glass?

_____ d. What was given to the seven angels?

Revelation 16

_____ a. What was the first plague and its effect? (See also Revelation 16:2a.)

_____ b. What was the second plague and its effect?

_____ c. What was the third plague and its effect?

_____ d. What was the fourth plague and its effect?

_____ e. What was the fifth plague and its effect?

_____ f. What was the sixth plague and its effect?

_____ g. What did the three unclean spirits do?

_____ h. What is the battle of Armageddon? (See Bible Dictionary, p. 614, s.v. "Armageddon.")

_____ i. What was the seventh plague and its effect?

Revelation 17

_____ a. What has become established throughout the earth? (See headnote to Revelation 17.)

_____ b. What did the angel show John?

_____ c. What have the kings and the inhabitants of the earth done? (See also Revelation 18:3.)

_____ d. What was the woman drunken with?

_____ e. Describe the beast that carried the woman.

_____ f. What do the seven heads of the beast symbolize?

_____ g. What do the ten horns of the beast symbolize?

_____ h. What are the waters where the whore sits?

_____ i. What will the ten horns of the beast do to the whore?

_____ j. What is the woman that John saw? (See also Revelation 17:18a.)

Revelation 18

_____ a. What did the angel say in Revelation 18:2–3? (See also headnote; Bible Dictionary, p. 618, s.v. "Babylon.")

_____ b. What did the voice in Revelation 18:4 tell the Saints to do? Why? (See also headnote.)

_____ c. What will happen to Babylon?

_____ d. Who will mourn when Babylon falls?

_____ e. Who were the merchants of Babylon?

_____ f. How were all nations deceived?

_____ g. What was found in Babylon?

Revelation 19

_____ a. What did the "great voice of much people" say in Revelation 19:1–2? (V. 1.)

_____ b. What is made ready? (See also headnote.)

_____ c. What is the fine linen mentioned in verse 8?

_____ d. What is the spirit of prophecy?

_____ e. What happened to the beast and the false prophet?

Revelation 20

_____ a. How long will Satan be bound? (See also headnote to Revelation 20.)

_____ b. Who will live and reign with Christ a thousand years?

_____ c. Why are they blessed who came forth in the first resurrection? (See also v. 6a.)

_____ d. Why will Satan be loosed for a short season at the end of the Millennium?

_____ e. Where will the devil be cast?

_____ f. How will we be judged?

_____ g. Who were cast into the lake of fire?

_____ h. What is the book of life? (See Bible Dictionary, p. 626, s.v. "Book of Life.")

Revelation 21

_____ a. What does the earth attain? (See headnote to Revelation 21.)

_____ b. What did John see in verses 1 and 2?

_____ c. Who will dwell with the Saints?

_____ d. Who are the sons of God who will inherit all things?

_____ e. What was the bride, the Lamb's wife?

_____ f. Describe the Lamb's wife.

_____ g. Why did the city not need the sun?

_____ h. Who will enter the holy city?

Revelation 22

_____ a. What will the Saints do? (See headnote to Revelation 22.)

_____ b. Who are blessed? (See also headnote.)

_____ c. What warning was given to those who would want to change the words of this prophecy?

Questions about Joseph Smith–Matthew

_____ a. What is the source of Joseph Smith–Matthew?

_____ b. What did the Lord's disciples understand about the Second Coming?

_____ c. What did Jesus prophesy in verse 3 about the destruction of Jerusalem in A.D. 70?

_____ d. What questions did the disciples ask Jesus?

_____ e. List five things Jesus told his disciples to do to prepare for the destruction of Jerusalem.

_____ f. List six events Jesus prophesied would precede the Second Coming.

_____ g. Why should we watch and prepare for the Second Coming?

_____ h. When will the end of the earth be? (See Bible Dictionary, p. 627, s.v. "By and By.")

Answers

Title Page
a. page i
b. page i

"To the Most High and Mighty Prince James . . . ": The Epistle Dedicatory
a. page iii
b. page iii–iv

The Names and Order of the Books of the New Testament
a. page v
b. page v

Explanation Concerning Abbreviations
a. page vi
b. page vi
c. page vi
d. page vi
e. page vi
f. page vi
g. page vi

Introduction to the Bible
Bible Dictionary

The Gospels
Bible Dictionary

Matthew

Introduction
Bible Dictionary

Matthew 1
a. Title
b. 16
c. 16e
d. 17

e. 19b
f. 20–21
g. 23

Matthew 2
a. Bible Dictionary
b. 2
c. 8
d. 11
e. 13
f. 16
g. 19–20
h. JST Matthew 3:24–26

Matthew 3
a. 1
b. 2–3
c. 2a
d. 5–6
e. JST Matthew 3:34–36
f. Bible Dictionary
g. 11
h. 15
i. 16–17

Matthew 4
a. 1b
b. 2c
c. 3–9
d. 11a
e. 17
f. 18–19
g. 20
h. 23

Matthew 5; 6; 7
a. Bible Dictionary
b. Bible Dictionary
c. Bible Dictionary

Matthew 5
a. 3a
b. 3–11
c. 13–15

d. 16
e. JST Matthew 5:21
f. 22
g. 39, 44–48

Matthew 6
a. 1–4
b. 2a
c. 6–7
d. 11–13
e. 14–15
f. 16–18
g. 19–21
h. 22
i. 24
j. 31–33

Matthew 7
a. 1a
b. 3–5
c. JST Matthew 7:9–11
d. JST Matthew 7:17
e. 12
f. 13–14
g. 15–20
h. 21
i. 24–27
j. 28–29

Matthew 8
a. 2–3
b. 5–10, 13
c. 14–15
d. 16
e. 26
f. 29

Matthew 9
a. 2a
b. 2
c. 6
d. 9
e. 9
f. 20–22
g. 27–30
h. 35

i. 36–38

Matthew 10
a. 1, 1b
b. 1
c. 2–4
d. 6–16
e. 18
f. 19–20
g. 28
h. 40–42

Matthew 11
a. 11
b. 14; JST Matthew 11:13–15
c. 20–22
d. 28–30

Matthew 12
a. 1–2
b. 3–8
c. 10–12
d. 24–30
e. 31–32
f. 33–35
g. 36–37
h. 38–39
i. 39–40
j. 50

Matthew 13
a. 10–16, 12a
b. 19
c. 19
d. 20–21
e. 22
f. 23
g. 37
h. 38
i. 38
j. 38
k. 39
l. 39
m. 40–43; JST Matthew 13:39–44

n. 47–50
o. 54–56
p. 57
q. 58

Matthew 14
a. 5
b. 3–4, 6–11
c. 21
d. 30–31
e. 35–36

Matthew 15
a. 7–9
b. 11, 17–20
c. 14
d. 28
e. 30–31
f. 32–39

Matthew 16
a. 12
b. 15–16
c. 17
d. 19
e. 21
f. 24d
g. JST Matthew 16:27–29
h. 27

Matthew 17
a. 1
b. 2
c. 3
d. 5
e. D&C 63:20–21
f. JST Matthew 17:14
g. 19–21
h. 27

Matthew 18
a. 3–4
b. 6
c. 15–17
d. 32–35

Matthew 19
a. 8
b. 16–21
c. 22
d. 28
e. 29

Matthew 20
a. 17–19
b. 26–28
c. 34

Matthew 21
a. 7–10
b. 12–13
c. 15
d. 21–22
e. 31–32
f. JST Matthew 21:51–53

Matthew 22
a. 18–21
b. 37–38
c. 39

Matthew 23
a. 3–8
b. 5
c. 7a, 8
d. 23
e. 28
f. 36a

Matthew 24
a. 4–5
b. 9
c. 11
d. 12
e. 14
f. 15–22
g. 24
h. 29–30
i. 30
j. 37–39
k. 44–47

Matthew 25
a. D&C 45:56–57
b. 3
c. 4
d. 13
e. 16
f. 20–21
g. 18, 24–25
h. 26–30
i. 33–45
j. 40
k. 41, 46

Matthew 26
a. 3–4

b. 14–16
c. 21–25
d. 26, 26b
e. 27–28; JST Matthew 26:24–25
f. 30
g. 39
h. 41
i. 56
j. 59
k. 63–66
l. 75

Matthew 27
a. 1–2
b. 3–5
c. 19
d. 20
e. 24
f. 25
g. 26–34
h. 39–43
i. 50a
j. 51–53
k. 57–60
l. 62–66

Matthew 28
a. 2a
b. 5–7
c. 9
d. 12–15
e. 18–20

Mark

Introduction
Bible Dictionary

Mark 1
a. Title
b. 3–8
c. 9–11
d. 12a
e. 13
f. 16–17
g. 18
h. 19–20
i. 32–34
j. 40–42

Mark 2
a. 3–12
b. 15
c. 17

d. JST Matthew 2:26–27

Mark 3
a. 1–4
b. 6
c. 10–11
d. 14–15
e. 23–26
f. 28–29

Mark 4
a. 14
b. 15
c. 16–17
d. 18–19
e. 20
f. 24–25
g. 31–32
h. 39–41

Mark 5
a. 7
b. 13
c. 18–19
d. 25–34
e. 37
f. 41

Mark 6
a. 2–3
b. 3
c. 4–6
d. 7–8
e. 13
f. 20
g. 17–28
h. 33–44
i. 55–56

Mark 7
a. 1–2
b. 6–8
c. 10–13
d. 18–23
e. 24a
f. 32–35

Mark 8
a. 1–3
b. Matt 16:12
c. 22–25
d. 29
e. 31

f. JST Mark 8:42–43

Mark 9
a. 2
b. 2–3
c. 4*a*
d. 7
e. 29
f. 34
g. 35
h. 42

Mark 10
a. 3–5
b. 6–12
c. 13–15
d. 16
e. 21
f. 27*a*
g. 32–34
h. 43–45
i. 51–52

Mark 11
a. 9–10
b. 15–17
c. 17–18
d. 24–26
e. 27–28
f. 29–33

Mark 12
a. 12
b. 12
c. 14–17
d. 27*a*
e. 29–30
f. 31
g. 38–40
h. 42–44

Mark 13
a. 5–26
b. 26–27
c. 32
d. 35–36

Mark 14
a. 1
b. 2
c. 8
d. 10–11
e. JST Mark 14:20–25
f. 30

g. JST Mark 14:36–37
h. JST Mark 14:38
i. 35–36
j. 44
k. 53
l. 56
m. 61–62
n. 64–65
o. 72

Mark 15
a. 1
b. 2
c. 10
d. 11
e. 16–20
f. 29–32
g. 34
h. 37–38
i. 40–41
j. 43, 46

Mark 16
a. 1–2
b. JST Mark 16:3–6
c. 9
d. 15–16
e. 17–18
f. 20

Luke

Introduction
  Bible Dictionary

Luke 1
a. Title
b. 1*a*
c. 1–2
d. 3
e. Bible Dictionary
f. 12
g. 13
h. 13–17
i. Bible Dictionary
j. 20
k. 26–27
l. 28–37
m. 38
n. 46–55
o. 67–79
p. 80

Luke 2
a. 1–5

b. 8–9
c. 10–12
d. 15–17, 20
e. 27–35
f. 40, 52
g. 46, 46*c*

Luke 3
a. 3
b. JST Luke 3:4–11
c. 9
d. 16–17
e. 19–20
f. 21–22
g. 23

Luke 4
a. 1
b. 2
c. 3–13
d. 28–29
e. 30
f. 34–36
g. 40
h. 44

Luke 5
a. 4
b. 6–7
c. 10
d. 12–13
e. 15
f. 20, 24
g. 30–32

Luke 6
a. 7–10
b. 11
c. 12
d. 13
e. 17
f. 20–22
g. 27–38
h. 38
i. 39
j. 41–42
k. 43–45
l. 47–48
m. 49

Luke 7
a. 9
b. 11–15
c. 23

d. 28
e. 50

Luke 8
a. 1
b. 2–3
c. 11
d. 12
e. 13
f. 14
g. 15
h. 25
i. 28
j. 46
k. 48
l. 54–55

Luke 9
a. 1
b. 2
c. 3–5
d. 11, 16–17
e. 22
f. JST Luke 9:24–25
g. 30
h. 31, 31*a*

Luke 10
a. 1
b. 5
c. 7–9
d. 17
e. 19
f. 20
g. 27
h. 36–37

Luke 11
a. 1
b. 4
c. 8–10
d. 23
e. 29
f. 34
g. 34–36
h. 39–44, 41*a*
i. 50–51
j. 52, 52*c*
k. 53–54

Luke 12
a. 2–3
b. 4–5
c. 8

d. 11–12
e. 16–21
f. 31, 31a
g. 34
h. 37–38
i. 47

Luke 13
a. 3, 5
b. 11–13
c. 14–16
d. 17
e. 28
f. 34

Luke 14
a. 5
b. 11
c. 12–14
d. 28–30, 30a

Luke 15
a. 7
b. 10
c. 31–32

Luke 16
a. 10
b. 13
c. 24, 27–28, 30
d. 25–26, 29, 31

Luke 17
a. 1–2
b. Matthew 18:15–17
c. 5
d. 15–19
e. 24
f. 26–30
g. JST Luke 17:38–40

Luke 18
a. 4–5
b. 6–8
c. 13–14
d. 17
e. 22–24
f. 27a
g. 31–33
h. 43

Luke 19
a. 6
b. 26

c. 37–38
d. 41–44
e. 47–48

Luke 20
a. 3–4
b. 5–6
c. 13–16
d. 19–20
e. 45–47

Luke 21
a. 4
b. 8
c. 8–24
d. 25–27, 25a
e. 36
f. 37–38

Luke 22
a. 2
b. 3–6
c. 19–20
d. 26–27
e. 32
f. 35
g. 42
h. 43
i. 60–62
j. 63–65
k. 66

Luke 23
a. 3
b. 20–24
c. 34
d. 46
e. 50–53

Luke 24
a. 1–4
b. 5–7
c. 12
d. 18–24
e. 30–31
f. 32
g. 36
h. 37–43
i. 46–50
j. 52–53

John

Introduction
  Bible Dictionary

John 1
a. Title

b. JST John 1:1–4
c. JST John 1:6–8
d. JST John 1:8–10
e. Moroni 7:16
f. 23
g. 29–34
h. 40–41
i. 45
j. 51

John 2
a. 4a
b. 6–11
c. 14–16
d. 21

John 3
a. 1–2
b. 5
c. 11–21, 11b
d. 16
e. 19–20
f. 36a

John 4
a. JST John 4:1–2
b. 13–14
c. 24
d. 25–26
e. 28–30
f. 39–42
g. 46–54

John 5
a. 16–18
b. 25, 28
c. 32a
d. 39

John 6
a. 2
b. 14
c. 15
d. 26
e. 38
f. 39–40
g. JST John 6:44
h. 68–69

John 7
a. 7
b. 17
c. 40–43

John 8
a. 5
b. 7
c. 10–11
d. 29
e. 31–32
f. 34
g. 40
h. 44
i. 47a
j. 58–59

John 9
a. 4–5
b. 16
c. 18–23
d. 30–33
e. 34
f. 35–38

John 10
a. 4–5
b. 10–11
c. 3 Nephi 15:11–24
d. 18
e. 37–38

John 11
a. 5
b. 16a
c. 17
d. 25–26
e. 27
f. 33–36
g. 43–46
h. 53–54

John 12
a. 5–6
b. 7a
c. 9–11
d. 16
e. 28
f. 30
g. 42–43
h. 49–50

John 13
a. 4–5
b. 14–15; JST John 13:10
c. 20
d. 27
e. 34

d. 13
e. 16
f. 22–23
g. 32–34

Acts 18
a. 1–3
b. 4
c. 5
d. 6
e. 9–10
f. 14–16
g. 19
h. 24–26
i. 27–28

Acts 19
a. 5–6
b. 11–12
c. 13–16
d. 19
e. 24–28
f. 35–41

Acts 20
a. 7a, 7d
b. 7–12
c. 11
d. 22–23
e. 24
f. 25–36
g. 29–30

Acts 21
a. 5
b. 10–11
c. 12
d. 13
e. 19
f. 27
g. 31–32

Acts 22
a. 3–5
b. 6–13
c. 17–18
d. 21
e. 22–23
f. 25–29

Acts 23
a. 3
b. 8
c. 8

d. 9–10
e. 11
f. 12–13
g. 16–22
h. 23–31

Acts 24
a. 1
b. 5–6
c. 10–21
d. 23
e. 24–25
f. 26–27

Acts 25
a. 1–3
b. 7
c. 9
d. 10–11
e. 13
f. 25–27

Acts 26
a. 2–3
b. 4–5
c. 9–11
d. 12–16
e. 17–18
f. 20–21
g. 24
h. 28
i. 29
j. 31–32

Acts 27
a. 3
b. 9–10
c. 18–20
d. 21–26
e. 33–34
f. 37
g. 41–44

Acts 28
a. 2
b. 3–6
c. 8–9
d. 17–20
e. 23
f. 24
g. 25–27
h. 30–31

The Epistles of Paul

Introduction
    Bible Dictionary

Romans

Introduction
    Bible Dictionary

Romans 1
a. 4
b. 7
c. 9–11
d. 16–17
e. 18
f. 19–20
g. 21–23
h. 24–27
i. 28–32

Romans 2
a. 1
b. 4
c. 6–10
d. 13
e. 17–20
f. 21–23
g. 29

Romans 3
a. Headnote, 20
b. Headnote, 24, 28
c. 1–2
d. 19

Romans 4
a. 3, 9
b. 16a
c. 16a
d. 24–25

Romans 5
a. 1
b. 3
c. 4
d. 4
e. 5
f. 6–8
g. 12–18
h. 18–19

Romans 6
a. 3–5
b. 12–14
c. 16
d. 17–18
e. 21, 23
f. 22–23

Romans 7
a. 4
b. JST Romans 7:5
c. 22

Romans 8
a. 6–8
b. 6
c. 14
d. 16–17
e. 28
f. 38–39

Romans 9
a. Headnote
b. 4
c. 31–32

Romans 10
a. 1–3, 21
b. 9–13
c. 16–17

Romans 11
a. Headnote, 5–7
b. Headnote, 16–24
c. Headnote, 25–27
d. 33–36

Romans 12
a. Headnote, 1
b. 2–3
c. 9–16
d. 17–21

Romans 13
a. Headnote
b. 1
c. 8
d. 12
e. 13–14

Romans 14
a. 10–13
b. 11
c. 17

Romans 15
a. 1–2, 5–7
b. 16–22
c. 30–32

Romans 16
a. 17–18

2 Peter 3
a. 3–4
b. 8
c. 9
d. 10; JST 2 Peter 3:10
e. 17–18

The Epistles of John

Introduction
    Bible Dictionary

1 John 1
a. 3
b. 5–7
c. 8, 10
d. 9

1 John 2
a. 1
b. 1, 1*a*, 1*b*
c. 3–6
d. 10
e. 15–17
f. 22

1 John 3
a. 2
b. 4
c. 12
d. 17
e. 18–21
f. 22

1 John 4
a. 1–3
b. 4
c. 7–11
d. 12*a*
e. 18
f. 20–21

1 John 5
a. Headnote, 1
b. Headnote, 10–13
c. 3
d. 13
e. 14–15

2 John 1
a. 4
b. 6

3 John 1
a. 4–6

b. 11

Jude

Introduction
    Bible Dictionary

Jude 1
a. 3
b. 4, 8, 10, 16
c. 6
d. 9
e. 14–15

Revelation

Introduction
    Bible Dictionary

Revelation 1
a. JST Rev 1:3
b. JST Rev 1:4
c. JST Rev 1:6;
    Headnote to
    Revelation 1
d. JST Rev 1:7
e. 13–16

Revelation 2
a. Headnote, 7, 11, 17,
    26
b. 2–3
c. 4–5
d. 10
e. 16
f. D&C 130:10–11
g. 20–25
h. JST Rev 2:26–27

Revelation 3
a. Headnote, 5, 12, 21
b. 2–4
c. 8–11
d. 15–19
e. 20

Revelation 4
a. Headnote
b. D&C 77:5
c. D&C 77:1
d. D&C 77:2–3
e. D&C 77:4

Revelation 5
a. 1, 9

b. D&C 77:6
c. 9
d. 11–14

Revelation 6
a. Headnote
b. D&C 77:7
c. 1–2
d. 3–4
e. 5–6
f. 7–8
g. Headnote, 9–11
h. Headnote, 12–17

Revelation 7
a. Headnote
b. D&C 77:8
c. D&C 77:9
d. 2–3, D&C 77:9
e. D&C 77:10
f. D&C 77:11
g. 13–14
h. 15–17

Revelation 8
a. Headnote
b. D&C 77:12

Revelation 9
a. Headnote
b. 3–4
c. 13–19
d. D&C 77:13

Revelation 10
a. Headnote
b. 3–4
c. 5–6
d. D&C 77:14
e. 11

Revelation 11
a. Headnote
b. 2
c. D&C 77:15
d. 3
e. 5–6
f. 7–10
g. 11–12
h. 13
i. 15
j. 16–17

Revelation 12
a. Headnote

b. JST Revelation 12:7
c. JST Revelation 12:7
d. JST Revelation 12:8
e. JST Revelation 12:11
f. JST Revelation
    12:12–13
g. JST Revelation 12:17

Revelation 13
a. Headnote, 1*a*
b. 5–7
c. 8
d. 14
e. 15
f. 16–17
g. 18

Revelation 14
a. Headnote, 1
b. Headnote, 6
c. 7
d. 8
e. 9–11
f. 13

Revelation 15
a. Headnote, 1
b. 2–4
c. 2
d. 7

Revelation 16
a. 2
b. 3
c. 4
d. 8–9
e. 10–11
f. 12
g. 13–14
h. 16; Bible Dictionary
i. 17–21

Revelation 17
a. Headnote
b. 1
c. 2
d. 6
e. 7
f. 9
g. 12–13
h. 15
i. 16
j. 18